Alessandro Dell'Acqua Alessandro Benedetti
Antonio Berardi Antonio Marras Blumarine Dolce & Gabbana
Emilio Pucci Etro Gianfranco Ferré Haute Kenzo by Antonio Marras
Mauzio Pecoraro Ricardo Risci Roberto Cavalli Valentino Versace

DAMIANI©2006

DAMIANI EDITORE via Zanardi, 376 - 40131 Bologna - Italy - Tel. +39.051.6350805 - Fax +39.051.6347188 - www.damianieditore.it - info@damianieditore.it
Author: Federico Rocca **Coordinators:** Marcella Manni, Giuseppe Villirillo **Artistic Direction:** Federico Rocca **Photographs:** Marco Ravenna, 2005
Digital file operator: Tiziano Menabò **Layout:** Federico Rocca, Lorenzo Tugnoli **Translation:** David Smith © **Texts:** Giusi Ferrè, Federico Rocca
© **Photographs:** Marco Ravenna, 2005
ISBN 88-89431-23-7
Printed on Magno Satin 170 gr. distributed by antalis™

The author would like to express his profound thanks to the following: Antonio Berardi, Consuelo Castiglioni, Eva Cavalli, Roberto Cavalli, Alessandro De Benedetti, Vincenzo De Cotiis, Alessandro Dell'Acqua, Domenico Dolce, Veronica Etro, Gianfranco Ferrè, Stefano Gabbana, Antonio Marras, Patrizia Marras, Anna Molinari, Maurizio Pecoraro, Laudomia Pucci, Rossella Tarabini, Riccardo Tisci, Valentino, Donatella Versace.
And also to: Stefania Alafaci, Cristina Bagnasacco, Stefania Baroni, Corinne Besquet, Dania Bianchini, Antonio Cappelli, Valeria Cerulli, Vito De Serio, Delphine Dichy, Federica Ernst, Fabio Feroce, Roberto Gino, Alfredo Girombelli, Milena la Gatta, Laurent Latko, Federica Marzi, Adrian James Mimnagh, Marcello Mosesso, Barbara Pedrini, Giovanni Perino, Pier Paolo Piccioli, Stefano Pitigliani, Giorgio Re, Marianovella Salvatori, Franco Santella, Lorenzo Serafini, Paolo Tarabini, Violante Valdettaro, Paul Warner, Lucia Zotti.

The author would also like to add particular thanks to Mrs Giorgia Rapezzi and Mr Jacopo Tonelli of JATO GROUP San Lazzaro di Savena (Bologna), who put their vast archives at our full disposal. Thanks also to their entire staff without whose precious help this book would not have been possible.

Lastly, the author wishes to express his most sincere gratitude to Mrs Giusi Ferrè.

Embroidery

Italian Fashion

Some people imagine clothes as uniforms for the daily war. Some see them as mirroring a social role. Some consign them to boredom and banality under the pretext of rationality. Some see them as punishment, lost in the sick game of punishments and the forbidden. And there are some who make a joyful gesture of every dress, a voyage through light and colour, a tremor of sensuality. Because dresses are embroidered, inlaid, billowing, hyper-decorated in a sweet chromatic and compositional anarchy that redefines the boundaries of taste. A feeling of the first day of creation flits through this fantastical world: the flowers of English wall-hangings and Victorian lace spring up in a tropical garden, magical animals lend the colours of their pelts, conceptual geometries open up new spaces, darting south sea fish have the splendour of unusual metals, butterfly wings blend in with the delicate venation of leaves.

Embroidery is a door open on a wondrous, opulent dimension where light plays with the richness of the threads. The modern violence of gesture transforms the substance of the material, like the burnt Swarovskis that are a hallmark of Riccardo Tisci. The ancient virtuosity of the lace-pillow is charged with emotion "as if," says Antonio Berardi, "it came directly from the diary of my life and memory".

Precious and sophisticated, embroidery is a timeless art which time renders increasingly rare due to the absolute dedication it requires – mental even more than physical – concentrated on the minuscule and the perfect, and to the infinite patience it demands, virtues that are so far from contemporary, so eccentric in a society that wants everything and wants it at once. This must be the reason why the lace-pillow dress that Antonio Berardi presented at his 1998 spring/summer collection is now in the Metropolitan Museum of New York. The other example is in the Museum of Offida, a small town in the Marches, famous for having been a centre for this type of work.

For three and a half months fourteen women worked to create this masterpiece, each making a certain part as if on an assembly line. With no stitching it had to be fitted directly onto Naomi Campbell's body using bone bobbins specially made for the purpose in England. The operation took more than forty-five minutes. The great thing about this 16th century marvel of patience is that it is Goth, punk, the expression of a wholly topical society and culture. No revival, no nostalgia but simply the taste for challenge, for impossible execution. Maurizio Pecoraro defines his "materic" obsession. And he explains: "More than working on the form of things I love to work in the material of things".

Micro-paillettes of 2 millimetres, mirrors, bugle beads, ribbons and very thin threads produce virtuosities, techniques, *coups de théâtre*, surprising elegances. As Maurizio Pecoraro explains in one of the fine interviews in this book that deal with the passionate relationship between fashion designers and embroidery: "women know that turning up at a party in an embroidered dress is quite different from arriving in an unembroidered… almost anonymous dress. Women feel richer wearing a decorated dress".

An embroidery may contain infinite feelings. We need only follow Antonio Marras' mental itinerary, expressed in a skirt presented at his first Milan show: from the memory of his father to Sardinian tradition and the presence of his children. And in fact the embroidery seems to allude to beginner's work: the gauze on which little girls once learned to embroider and sew with clumsy stitches until experience taught them precision and care. Marras asked the embroiderers to imitate this style, calling it "wrongstitch". And these extraordinary women, accustomed to perfection, learned just what feeling, what fascination can be concealed in an apparent mistake. Which actually became one of the post-modern languages of embroidery.

INTRODUCTION

The 1980's came and went, leaving their mark. And how. On fashion perhaps more indelibly than elsewhere. On Italian fashion certainly more indelibly than elsewhere.

Useless to deny, impossible to forget.

We all remember well the furores of that decade without limits and without rules (or with too many?). We remember them well and it isn't just a question of nostalgia. It's that we found them once more before our eyes, and in the magazines and on the catwalks, even on the streets, less than twenty years later, not even the physiological time of a generation. Some people loved them and still do, others hated and violently attacked them.

However we want to consider them, those years were certainly not, as they may have then appeared, a big hallucinated soap bubble, light and inconsistent, weightless and without demands, ready to dissolve with a gust of wind.

The 80's came and went, and if we really wanted to give them an official point of departure it could be a date: 29th July 1981. A symbolic date, symbol of an epoch. Lady Diana Spencer, projected onto the screens of eight hundred million tele-dreamers, married Prince Charles in St Paul's cathedral. The future queen of Hearts was enclosed in an ivory silk taffeta dress, costing nine thousand pounds at the time, created by David and Elizabeth Emanuel. Embellished with old lace, wide puffed sleeves curled with tiny silk ribbons, a train more than seven metres long, with crystal, diamonds, pearls, beads and bows as if they had rained down. The world's tabloids carried a front page (royal) family portrait. In the centre of the group, the white cloud of the dream dress. It's the photo of that epoch and of the fashion that would shortly "rise up". Let's focus. Let's zoom in. Let's enlarge a detail.

The 80's came and went, clean and clear albeit mobile and fleeting. A whole decade – maybe the last century's longest and most excessive – of luxurious and luxuriant extremisms, of baroque and neo-baroque exaggerations, of romantic and new romantic excesses, of pirate-like and fairytale disguises, of ingenious tightrope walking between ironic hedonistic inclinations and highly serious social-climber, careerist, individualist and yuppy imperatives. There was ostentation, opulence, there was an insane, carcinogenic, merciless narcissism. There was a deafening, endless shout: *gimme more*! Appearing for the sake of appearing was imposed. There was the Eldorado of the possible egocentric satisfaction of need and, especially, of dream. There were the material girls and career women dressed for success, Dallas and Dynasty. There was, in brief, a powerful river in spate of bold and ruling 'isms', exciting, rigidly codified trends of ways and wearing, as ironbound as laws and as impassable as barbed wire frontiers. You were either in or out. But you *had to be* in. Also, and above all, in the fashion world. Never as in that decade have trends followed one on the other and been stratified so violently and rapidly. Never as in that decade, probably, have the various trends linked by the fashion system made themselves universally imperative at every possible user level, from palace to pavement, from riches to rags. Never as in that decade have the multiform avenues traced out by Fashion been able to absolutely dominate everything that gravitated around the fashion Industry. Including the high craft of embroidery. Over all those years embroidery had been fundamentally experienced as a form of ornament and decoration – one among many – which could be extensively used. Literally, extensively abused. Bent to the needs of the moment and circumstances, embroidery became servant and subject of the rule-breaking oddities of the various circumvolutions imposed by the evolution of fashions and tastes. So embroidery was the object and instrument of hyper-decorative frenzies, a means of ornamental hyper-trophies, and by the end – both time and logic wise – of the parabola of Eighties taste, even a battering ram to enter the territories of the descent into kitsch hyperbolism. Embroidery followed fashion as the rats followed the Pied Piper, and inevitably fell (off) into the gorge of what, *a posteriori*, would be stamped as bad taste (only to be rehabilitated, revamped and almost immediately contested less than twenty years later …).

Having emerged more or less undamaged from the great catastrophes of the second half of the decade (the wildfire spreading of AIDS in '85, the apocalypse of Chernobyl in '86 and the Stock Exchange crashes of '87), the impudently noisy optimism of international fashion seemed to stop only when faced with the rubble, also coloured, of the Berlin Wall. You noted something new in the air, though it was difficult to say what. Something you didn't understand, and hence also scary. It was only the first Gulf War (1990/91) that rationally justified this fear and put a definitive stop to everything the Eighties had meant, also in the fashion world: unconditioned optimism, unlimited consumerism, immodest amassing of wealth.

Force majeure or the simple, inevitable, cyclical inversion of taste? Hard to say. Certainly a parenthesis was opened. Which lasted slightly less than a decade.

Someone threw the switch. Pulled out the plug. The sparkling gleam of strass and sequins (the thousand lights of New York, to put it à la McInerney) which had shone for over a decade suddenly, almost unexpectedly, went out. A blanket of neutralising darkness was laid with the lightness of a rock on fashion and on fashion folks' ways. Minimalism had arrived. The diktat of *less is more*. The iconoclastic rage for *understatement* had arrived. A courageous army of fashion designers took up the ideals of sobriety, simplicity and linearity of a certain type of American art and literature. Those were the years of Prada and Jill Sander, of an Armani still abreast of the times, of Helmut Lang. The fashion system crowned the *basic* as a winning trend. The true essence became absence. Even fashion became spiritual, immaterial and ascetic. Mystical and wholly interior. Zen. Buddhism became a fashion, and followers of fashion dressed up as metropolitan Buddhists.

The colours on the catwalks were natural. Whites, blacks and "rule-breaking" touches of beige. The fabrics were simple (whether hyper-technological or raw didn't change anything) and the cut rigorous. Few decorations. Don't overdo the spangles. Don't dare the glitter of a paillette. Woe betide you if you risk any embroidery more elaborate than a barely hinted at thread. In the name of the delicacy of plainness, embellishment was banned. For some this was all modern and sophisticated. For others it was just sad. In fact a reaction (or revolution) wasn't slow in coming.

Minimalism also came to an end. Pure coincidence, certainly. But the same Lady D. mentioned above died on 31st August 1997. More or less when Minimalism died. The princess who, alone, had crowned herself queen of the people and icon of style, who could switch from shimmering evening gowns to (apparently) anonymous T-shirts, once more reflected the spirit of the times. Another photograph, obscenely talked about by many and (fortunately) seen by few. The one of Lady Diana Spencer breathing her last, caged in the crushed metal of her Mercedes. The princess was wearing very simple cream-coloured tube trousers and an even simpler dark jacket over a black top. At the time of her death the princess was in perfect harmony with the minimalist Zeitgeist.

Minimalism also came to an end, and its end did not leave space for many compromises. As if half-measures really weren't fashionable. A sudden passage from nothing to everything. From whisper to scream. From Minimum to Maximum.

Minimalism also came to an end, and the watershed was Gucci's 1999 spring/summer menswear collection designed by Tom Ford. Strawberry or wisteria pink trousers – decorated with flamboyant Swarovski crystals and glittering drops of glass – shocked, scandalised and immediately conquered. The jeans version, embroidered with large oriental-style flowers, was brought out the following season. The seed of Maximalist taste was sown in the fertile soil of a society that had rediscovered the desire to consume, and in the years to come there would be a flowering of trends and countertrends bursting like crazed shrapnel. The trail was blazed. The trail of the Much, the Lots, sometimes the Too Much. All the others slipped into the open wake. At the turn of the millennium the new buzzwords were eclecticism, intermingling, mixing, fusion, melting pot, pastiche, *métissage*. Also in fashion. On the catwalks you saw everything and the contrary of everything. Even simultaneously. Styles multiplied in bunches, trends were propagated exponentially. Barriers between styles and tastes were created only to be broken down at once. There were no laws, or perhaps there were so many that nobody felt duty bound to codify and obey them to the letter. Perhaps there were suggestions. All in the name of a presumed freedom achieved. Giorgio Gaber sang *"libertà, libertà obbligatoria"* (freedom, compulsory freedom). Surprised spectators, we witnessed a procession of gipsy and new hippy, of conceptual and cyberpunk, of nude look and military, of ethnic and retro, of girlie and de-constructivism, of urban sport and techno-fashion, of neo-romantic and heroin chic… The rules of consumer capitalism imposed a wearying, very rapid regeneration of fashions and styles. Which got mixed, added on, superimposed, cancelled out, included and incorporated in a great confusion. So much so that a doubt arose. And the doubt was: but can these trends of new millennium fashion be real ones? Aren't they rather just handy definitions for the effects, use and consumption of glossy paper? Do they differ so much – in lack of discipline and rigidity – from those of the Eighties? It was a legitimate doubt, resolved only by resignation to a given fact. Which is to say that all those listed above (and all the many others left unmentioned) were not actual trends. The real post-minimalist macro-trend (if there was one), transversal and underlying all the other handy definitions that fashion had come up with in recent seasons, was luxury (even more than show). The pleasure of richness and/or abundance returned. At top levels, luxury was expressed in both the "how" and in the "how much" dimension. There was a resurgence of the taste for opulence. The fascination with exclusiveness returned. With special series. With limited editions. With one-off pieces. Luxury was subdivided into all its accepted and disparate meanings. One of these – certainly not the only one but perhaps the most important and exploited, and definitely the one that interests us – was decor, embellishment, ornament. The great Made in Italy masters, no less than the young designers who were overwhelmingly approaching the fashion system, went back to increasing and increasingly imaginative use of decoration, not only as complement or completion but very often as the cutting edge, the backbone, the load bearing architrave of their creations.

Embroidery and application took on an absolutely leading role within this orientation. Embroidery actively made fashion and did not follow it (running behind, enslaved to its various ramifications) as it had done twenty years earlier. Now fashion had to adapt to the creativity and talent of embroidery. Now it was embroidery that called the tune, and the variables of fashion danced a rondo around it. Embroidery became the fulcrum, a Sun around which the planets of styles and customs gravitated. Increasingly often a dress was cut and sewn around an idea of decoration. Democratisation and globalisation also involved the world of embroidery, which expanded in every sphere and at every level of clothing, even breaking into the austere male wardrobe and overflowing copiously onto street market stalls. Thus demonstrating the fact that a fashion may be transformed into a phenomenon of custom. And not only: embroidery expanded its boundaries, becoming "anything" that could enrich and embellish an article of clothing. Any material, any technique the imagination could come up with, became an instrument of decoration to such an extent that it might be more correct to replace the term "embroidery" with "application".

With the urgent need to continually renew and regenerate their sources of inspiration, frenetically, it was natural and inevitable that the creativity of fashion designers – with regard to the use and inventiveness of embroidery – should turn towards an Elsewhere (spatial, cultural and above all temporal) whose frontiers extended without limit. Indiscriminately every epoch, every culture, every ravine of the globe became an inexhaustible well of possible sources of inspiration and influence. Creative seductions and evocations could be discovered literally anywhere. The important thing, the thing that created the swerve towards talent, invention, art, lay simply in the designers' skill in passionately knowing what they intended to manipulate, knowing how to reinterpret it with taste, and their desire to reinvent it with genius. This is the aesthetics of *repêchage*. The aesthetics that this book aims to illustrate. With the images and words of those who have been its advocates, followers and adepts.

A final click, perhaps, as someone has said, when time is up. The flashbulbs go off hallucinated and impress on film the outline of a damasked topcoat, designed by Robinson Valentine, in porcelain blue with a short train completely decorated with delicate hand embroidery in various shades of gold thread and a crown of ears of corn (or thorns). The photo made all the front pages on 10th April 2005. The woman wearing it was called Camilla. But that really is quite another Story...   FEDERICO ROCCA

INTERVIEW with Giorgia Rapezzi

Almost forty years in the fashion world. At the end of the Sixties, an inquisitive and enthusiastic researcher, fascinated by the European avant-gardes, importing to Italy the freshest and newest waves of what was happening on both sides of the English Channel. Then from the Seventies a successful fashion designer with her own brand (first Giorgia Fashion and then Giorgia per Sigheja) of modern, original lines, as well as consultant for important prêt à porter brands. For twenty years Giorgia Rapezzi has been the creative head of Jato, a leading European embroidery factory that offers consultancy and production services to the greatest and liveliest names in national and international fashion. Today it is certainly a point of reference for anyone – in Italy or abroad – who wants to learn about, use and interpret embroidery. In these decades Giorgia Rapezzi has fully earned her reputation as embroidery expert.

This interview gives us insight – through a simultaneously insider and outsider eye – into what embroidery has been and represented in this past decade of Italian fashion. Both player and spectator. The eye of someone who has seen fashion in the making from very close-up, the succession of trends and the evolution of taste. But also someone who has been able and has wanted to observe – with the right detachment – from a privileged position. An eye at once critical and affectionate.

I started working with embroidery in India in 1984 and I've never stopped. I was immediately surprised by the extraordinary talent of Indian embroiderers: I discovered exceptional manual skill that could make embroidery a highly refined art. But they followed canons of taste that were deeply rooted in the culture and style of the country, and therefore miles away from the orientations of European taste. So I realised I'd have to teach those craftspeople to work in full respect of their age-old traditions but in a completely different spirit, making them and their mastery an indispensable and very precious resource for Italian creativity, and not only Italian. I worked on embroidery frames, side by side with Indian craftspeople. This led to reciprocal exchange of the riches of their culture and ours, their technical skill and our aesthetic sensitivity. I tried to make their very ancient tradition suitable for the contemporary west. Nothing more.

I then began meeting the great designers and hearing their ideas. I just wanted to put myself and my company, Jato, at their service, and to carry on my work, always coherently and always to the best of my abilities. I tried in those years to translate the designers' thoughts into reality. I gave concreteness to their imaginations, I brought their desires to life. That was and is my job.

Easy to say but hard to do, I imagine. How do you manage to give concrete form to what designers want?

By taking their ideas, respecting them and working on them. Making their natural evolution possible. I'm given an idea and my task is to make it blossom; I'm given a thought and I transform it into embroidery. In a certain sense I'm a translator: I translate ideas into beads, paillettes, thread and whatever else the mind and imagination can contemplate. Within the limits of my possibilities, I've been the hand of designers' minds.

You've been involved with embroidery for twenty years and had the luck to experience it before, during and after Minimalism, which was probably the real, great, epoch-making revolution in world fashion in recent decades. From your privileged vantage point, what do you think the big differences are in the embroidery of these three different periods? And what about its evolution?

I've neither seen nor experienced such a violent and traumatic evolution. As far as embroidery is concerned, Minimalism wasn't an actual breaking point or substantial change of course. And there's an explanation for this: we should never forget that the concept of embroidery – in the vast ocean of fashion and its unwritten laws – is in itself a strange and absolutely atypical thing. And then, embroidery isn't so subject to the imperatives of the moment, of trends. It's somehow a timeless thing, outside history. Embroidery is the elaboration of a material. I think that's the best definition of "embroidery". It's wrong to think of it as just the glimmer of stones, strass or paillettes. Erroneously understood in this way, embroidery is certainly slave to the alternate phases and periods of fashion, and its respectability and good fortune will go up and down intermittently. But considered in its broader and truer aspect, embroidery is simply the working of a material to be applied to a garment with view to creating emotion. Any work process whatever: this is fundamental, because embroidery can and must use all kinds of material, transforming it through any type of elaboration imaginable. Setting out from this different point of departure it's easy to see how embroidery and decoration, even during minimalism, enjoyed extraordinary importance, maybe actually greater than in the previous and subsequent years. I worked an awful lot even in the mid 90's, focusing my work and attention on touches, details, finishes... It was highly sophisticated work, difficult and demanding, precisely because it wasn't aimed at emphasising the evident but rather at adding value to the scarcely perceptible. Think of Prada at that time, their tiny handbags. There was embroidery – and how! It was certainly different, but it was there. Embroidery can change in modes and modalities, but in substance, which is to say in its essence, it always remains the same and faithful to itself. This is its strength, this is what makes it indispensable.

Embroidering is like painting. You may be a convinced hyperrealist or an extreme abstractionist, but you are still a painter and your creation is a painting. That's how it is with embroidery. Because with the technique of embroidery you can express yourself just as you like. The important thing is to succeed in transforming material into emotion. The important thing is that embroidery can transform a simple dress into a dream, or better, into a desire. In painting, the materials are oil, tempera or water colours. In embroidery… they may be virtually anything. The greatness of embroidery lies in the fact that it embraces an extraordinary quantity of concepts and possibilities.

But then it becomes hard to set limits, to set boundaries between embroidery and what is no longer embroidery...

Just as it should be. There shouldn't be any limits or boundaries. I think I've ranged around quite a bit, and I'd like to think I've still got a lot of ranging to do. What I really like is experimenting with new materials. I've worked with all kinds of material in the past, even with electrical coils that I got from England… But the same thing goes for sculpture. In antiquity they used bronze and marble almost exclusively. At a certain point sculptors began using any material that ingenuity could come up with. There are actually artworks today made with little plastic containers. And admirers say: ah, this is modern! I believe that it's a peculiarity of modern art to consider all kinds of material noble and useable.

Embroidery is often seen as something démodé, antique, old… Are you saying that the choice of a special material can also make an embroidery modern?

Certainly. The designer gives you an input and you make your suggestion, but if you really want to go beyond, to go farther ahead, you have to experiment, especially with materials, in such a way that the customer's wish is suited and adapted to the time we're living in. You have to do things in such a way, substantially, that a piece of embroidery has a contemporary fascination. We very often draw inspiration from antique embroidery, a widespread practice and work method in recent years, and very stimulating. This kind of research has become one of Jato's strong points. You find stuff on your travels, at street markets or in shops selling vintage material. But the basic thing is to succeed in elaborating antique pieces in a way that makes them contemporary. This goes for every season and aspect of fashion.

So if an embroidery is to be beautiful it must, fundamentally, be a modern one …
Exactly.

You were talking about painting and sculpture. As if you wanted to put embroidery under the heading of art rather than its usual heading of high or very high craft …
If I had time I could make it art, but at the moment the customers think about turnover… Joking apart, I believe that under certain circumstances, when certain magical things happen, it can really be art. It has all the necessary possibilities and potentialities. Like painting and sculpture, it's a very ancient means of expression … I don't see any striking differences between these means of expression.

Two very important and often interconnected concepts frequently come up when speaking about embroidery: on the one hand luxury, and on the other hand richness and opulence. Where do you think embroidery stands between those two poles?
The opening premise is that luxury and richness aren't always in step. Indeed the two concepts are very often absolutely separate, they clash and don't sit well together at all. Luxury may also be highly concealed. Luxury may be allowing oneself to have a personality. Luxury is a sensation that is not proper to the object in itself but to the eye of the beholder and the attitude of the wearer. Richness is something else. It's clearer, more evident. Shameless if you like. Luxury is an intimate thing while richness is something displayed. Embroidery may succeed very well in uniting these two things, but not always. Nor should it be taken for granted that they must always be united.

The past ten years have been defined, among other things, as "the new luxury decade". Could you sketch me out a map of embroidery over the last ten years? An overview, your sampling… what has embroidery been and represented for Italian fashion in these years?
I don't know… I don't know what embroidery has represented in the last ten years… it's so hard to give an answer. The only thing I'm sure about is that it's been extensively photographed by the press, because it's very photogenic!

Is that all?
I don't know. I've worked and done little else, trying to do my job the best I can. But I must admit that I haven't seen any great embroidery evolution or revolution.

Have there been more macroscopic trends – more easily identifiable and definable – in the last ten years of Italian embroidery?
As always in fashion, there have been cycles. Seasons of thread-only embroidery, seasons of paillettes, etc. etc…
I'd say in general that this decade has been decidedly consecrated to the obvious and the clamorous. So for women there was great emphasis on sensuality. The buzzword was "sexy". The style of Cavalli

and his followers took over. This was the taste embraced by the masses, in the best conception of the term. The woman of this decade is striking, she wants to be there, be seen, heard and also desired. She wants at all costs to display a femininity which often, however, is not real Femininity understood as the essence of the female. I find a lot of confusion about terms in the world of women. The fashion of this decade believes it has exalted femininity but I really can't agree with that. A certain idea of woman was imposed, which in my opinion was incorrect or at any rate extremely partial. Women don't yet know their own dictionary, and perhaps fashion somewhat takes advantage of the fact. Whereas fashion should also help women to understand and know themselves, to increase awareness of their own being.

What do you think of the label Maximalism as applied to the fashion of the last ten years?

We Italians, or maybe I should say we Europeans, live in a cultural environment imbued for centuries by the concept of richness. The 17th century was the golden age for all European nations, the Baroque age. European taste is constitutionally, but also historically, baroque taste: decoration, embellishment, opulence, abundance and splendour. Throughout Europe highly decorated churches and palazzos rose up at every crossroads, in every square. Minimalist taste isn't indigenous to us. Or better, we assimilated it and were also able to interpret it well, but it doesn't spring from our culture. It's something from outside, imported, that does not belong to us. We took it from the Americans who in turn had taken it from the Japanese… Over the years and with the evolutions of style and fashion our true nature often resurfaces in spite of our efforts to camouflage, subjugate or domesticate it. A European may feel great in a house furnished entirely with Eames and Knoll pieces, but only for a very short time… After a while the need to add something emerges imperiously: a big lamp, a special curtain, a carpet… European taste isn't simple. In this sense the definition Maximalism given to the European fashion of the past ten years corresponds to an undeniable truth that also stands outside history. In Europe, decoration is something deeply cultural, even more than social. We belong to a baroque world, our very mentality is baroque in its reasoning capacities… Confirmation of this propensity lies in the fact that those centuries and periods of opulence, richness and splendour are always, cyclically, taken as an example and model of inspiration for current fashion. Because they're periods that excite, surprise, always produce an effect, a disturbance, a thought. And they're also periods that allow today's fashion to put its foot right down on the experimentation pedal. Something I feel is indispensable.

So you feel we can't talk at the moment about an imminent return of Minimalism as has been suggested in certain press items? Or at least not in the strictest sense of the term... More generally, how do you see the immediate and long term future of embroidery?

I reaffirm the concept: I think there's a need for experimentation, but at the moment there's little desire or courage to go ahead. It seems to me a moment in which trends are followed too much, without the knowledge of how to reinvent them or make them your own. Whereas the true function of genius is to subvert trends, to try and go against them. True genius is what mixes up the cards, breaks things up, contradicts and burns bridges. It goes against mainstream thought, seeks alternative possibilities of information. There aren't many geniuses around nowadays. Either that or nobody wants to risk much to prove that they are one. And this is a pity, because embroidery is an instrument which if correctly understood – meaning the possibility of bringing a material to life by giving it an unusual form – allows almost limitless possibilities for experimentation. With embroidery you can obtain effects that are unachievable with just fabrics, cuts or anything else. With embroidery you can do everything, everything you want to do. All you need is the courage to take up this challenge. All you need to do is to welcome excess when all the others are bowing down to rigour. Embroidery is the access key to genius in fashion.

But there's great uncertainty in fashion today. Nobody wants to run the risk of taking up a clear position, so everybody plods along trying to keep one foot here and one there, waiting to see which way the wind blows before hoisting sail.

In fifty years what will be left of the embroidery of these years?

Certainly some pieces here and there on flea-market stalls, sought by designers for inspiration and bought at high prices. Exactly what I do today, buying 20's and 30's stuff. History, especially in fashion, always repeats itself. Moreover, there has always been decoration in all phases of history and in the evolution of fashion and costume. Even in the minimalism we discussed earlier. Even in the 60's: maybe it was a different decoration, maybe a dress had ten paillettes, but they were gigantic à la Paco Rabanne. There has always been decoration, in every season of fashion bar none. I'd say that you can't have fashion without decoration. This goes for men as much as women. Of course the methods are different, but I believe the intensity and desire are the same. If you're unaware of this and want to be convinced, just have a glance at past centuries. The evidence of the 18th century alone is enough to bear out the truth of this thought.

But why do women really love and seek decoration? What has urged them down through the ages to desire and wear decorated clothes, in different ways depending on the epoch but always and in any case decorated?

Because they're repressed. Women have always felt set aside by the male world and have inevitably suffered from this. In the early centuries of the first millennium a pope ordered women to wear low-cut dresses and display their breasts in order to attract the distracted eyes of men who absolutely no longer paid attention to women. The situation now is more or less the same, perhaps even taken to its extreme. If women want to be noticed, considered and maybe even loved they have to attract men's attention, also with these means. Also with an embroidered dress. For centuries women have done their utmost to arouse men's interest. This seems to be their sad fate.

The inspiration for this garment has varied origins. Clearly we set out from old African cushions. But there's also the influence of bori, antique Japanese patchworks made by peasants in the poorest rural areas of the country who put together pieces of old clothes... A few years ago someone applied these bori to a support, creating works of art that somehow recalled Alberto Burri, and then had them auctioned at exorbitant sums. Those inspirations from different cultures and epochs found a point of convergence in this embroidery.   VERONICA ETRO

Embroidery is important only if it succeeds in telling the same story I want to tell in my fashion design. But it isn't fundamental. It's an accessory. In fact some of my collections include embroidery while others do not.

In the case of this collection, for example, embroidery was necessary.

In devising my collections I proceed as if I were building a character for a film. Fashion as I practise it is somehow a sort of film. Everything starts at the moment when I create, invent, a character, just like a scriptwriter who has to breathe life into the protagonist of the film he has in mind. Once the character has come into focus I wonder what she might wear. If the character in the imaginary script I have in my head is someone who would wear embroidered clothes then I'm more than happy to comply. Otherwise, if embroidery doesn't suit the character and the story I want to tell, I can do very well without it. I don't feel the need to use embroidery always and in all cases. I really use it as if it were an accessory: not under all circumstances, not at all times do we have to wear a necklace or a hat. Similarly, to my mind, a dress doesn't always need embroidery.

I decide to use embroidery when I see that it's coherent with what I'm doing. In this sense Rossella Tarabini style embroidery could be defined as "useful". Although we are probably talking about the most useless thing in the world. Embroidery is useful in its uselessness.

In the case of this dress, and this collection in general, embroidery was absolutely functional. I set out from a drawing of Marchesa Casati dressed as an American Indian and from the concept of Orientalism as understood in the Twenties, when the English went to India and reproduced European style clothes with Indian fabrics. I used the word "Indian" and the concept of Orientalism, but transported them into the world and culture of the American Indians. I wanted to create Twenties style embroideries in European taste, but with the naïf charm of American Indian work. I'm not able, for example, to do things of strictly ethnic inspiration, so even materials like shells and mother-of-pearl – today normally associated with ethno-folk taste – were used following principles of purely European taste.

With this collection I enjoyed tackling a particular creative process in devising the embroidery, but with the awareness and certainty that I'll never use it again. The mental process that lies behind the creation of a piece of embroidery is never the same in my fashion design. Or better: it's always different in order to be always the same. You change in order not to change… Even with embroidery I think I always do exactly the same thing actually. While I'm working on the collections I realise that I always like the same things and colours.

Put simply, I try each time to find a different scenario for the story I want to tell. ROSSELLA TARABINI for ANNA MOLINARI

This skirt has a slightly unusual history. My father had a draper's shop which, towards the end of the Seventies, was turned into a clothes shop. I kept, and still possess, the bolts of cloth that were left in the warehouse. When I came to do my first prêt à porter show in Milan I decided to use a piece of that cloth to create a skirt. Maybe it was a touch-wood gesture, maybe a sign of acknowledgement to my father, or maybe it was just because the bright green contrasted well with the rest of the collection which was very gloomy, very black… I don't really know why myself. But the really curious thing is that the embroidery is made up of a series of many tiny pieces of applied fabric, forming a sort of design. These were cut up by my kids who have a desk in my studio and enjoy themselves cutting and pasting and assembling bits of fabric… The fragments of cloth cut out and composed by my kids were then organised and applied by the women who work with me.

This skirt is also important because it marked the beginning or the broadening of a job of recovery with regard to a craft embroidery tradition we wanted to resuscitate and give new life to. We rediscovered the extraordinary craftwork and manual skills of the Sardinian women of Ittiri, embroiderers by tradition. This tradition was on its way out, or at least was limited to creating articles for personal use. We somehow recovered the tradition but also overturned it. I asked these women to create, imagine and seek an absolutely crazy kind of embroidery, totally unusual for them. They were accustomed to the "rules", to making every stitch exactly, precisely, perfectly and almost maniacally identical to the others. What I asked them to do was to invent a new one to which I gave the name "wrongstitch". The effect was supposed to be like the embroidery of a child who takes up needle and thread and starts sewing. That's what I tried to do for the first time, "messing around" with this skirt and waiting to see what might happen. These women were thrown into confusion. They really couldn't conceive of or execute those distorted, irregular and imprecise stitches. Then after trial and error we got it right. We succeeded in getting this new cycle off the ground.

This skirt is absolutely important and special to us. It speaks of my father, myself and the Sardinian tradition. But above all of my children. Their creativity is precious to me. Everything they draw, create or make is filed and kept jealously in a drawer. An incredible source of inspiration.

This skirt also marks a moment in which I rediscovered memory. Each time I create my collection I feel the need, the necessity, to tell a story. As if I were writing a film script. And the story I tell almost always has a melodramatic if not expressly dramatic vein. It's part of my tormented, agonized nature. In films too I detest a happy ending and I detest comedies. I'm really drawn to tormented things, be they films, music, images… I adore things that correspond to my melodramatic side. And in the same way I love to tell, in my collections, stories that have the same tone. Maybe this is why I love talking about and elaborating memory. Because memories are often tormented.   ANTONIO MARRAS

I had an uncle who emigrated to Argentina. He made a fortune and become the classic rich uncle. He was a very handsome and elegant man. An elegance which belongs only to the men of that period. His jackets and suits were made by Italian tailors who had emigrated to Argentina. Clothes of absolute refinement.

On his death his estate was bequeathed to various nephews and nieces. Among other things, I inherited his wardrobe. This very strange thing would have made any other person angry, but I believe that nothing happens by chance in life. I was extremely pleased to own his wardrobe. I believe in destiny, in the fact that things happen because they were intended to happen and that from every fortuitous encounter or circumstance something good may emerge. This wardrobe consisted of beautiful things: white shirts, jackets, suits, overcoats... Among these things there was a jacket somewhat more worn out than the others. I started off by washing it, and the cloth became matted. Then the sleeve linings came away and even the sleeves got unstitched. So we decided to reline it with vintage fabrics, and then added first paillettes and then applications... In a short time this jacket, originally very masculine and severe, became an absolutely different female garment. ANTONIO MARRAS

This collection was inspired by Atlantis, and therefore by the sea. The material of this bodice attempts, precisely, to reproduce sea-urchins. ANTONIO MARRAS

Antonio Marras, s/s 2005

32

This skirt originated with a pair of trousers I inherited from my uncle. I like using second hand clothes as a departure point for my creations. I like to manipulate garments already lived in by other bodies, in which other people have spent time. Garments already stroked by other hands, well worn, maybe badly treated. Garments which in any case have already lived one or more lives, one or more histories. I really like telling the story of things already possessed or known. I like things with experience, not only clothing but everything around me: places, objects, furniture…

This skirt was part of a collection dedicated to female mineworkers. Until just a few years ago there was a fairly lively mining tradition in Sardinia. The prohibitive costs of this type of extraction led to its decline. That economy also involved women and children who worked under tough conditions. The women's job was sorting: they had to select, break and bag the minerals extracted from the mine. We wanted to tell this story. The story of these women who in their work got burns not only on their hands but also on their clothes. So they wore burnt, patched, torn and stained dresses that showed all the signs of the wear and tear of work. This skirt aims to recreate and imagine all the sparkle of stones and metals, gold and silver adhering to the train and taken away from the mine by the women leaving their workplace.   ANTONIO MARRAS

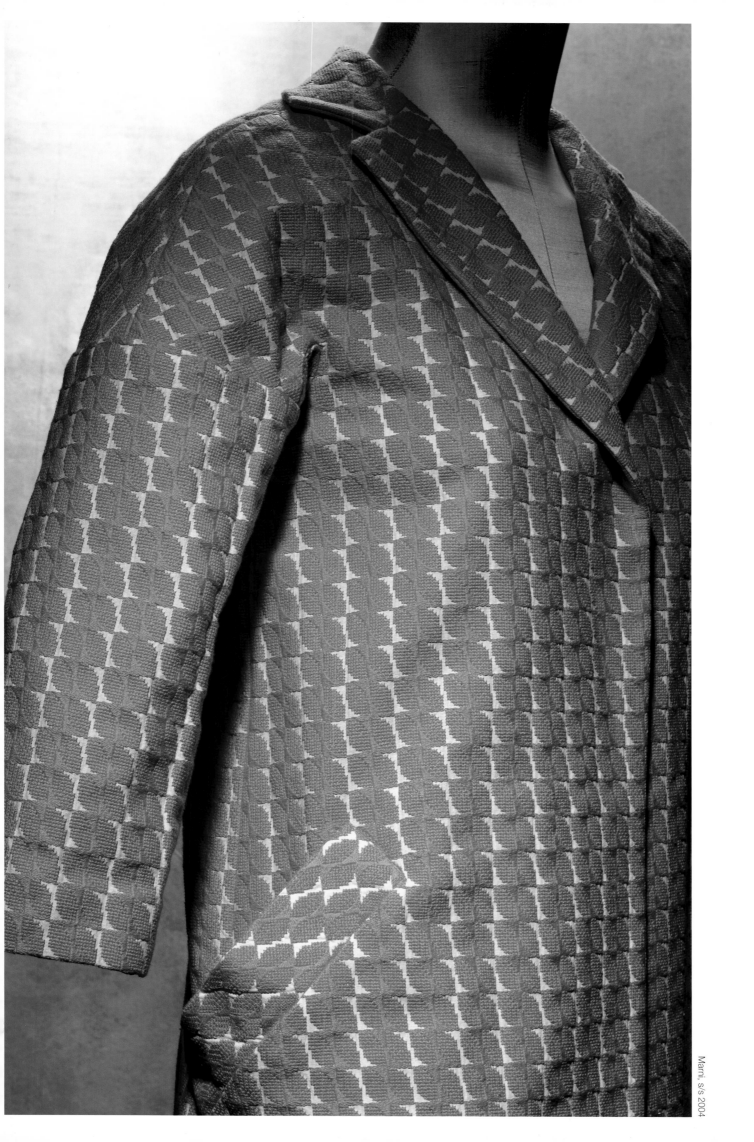

The embroidered fabric makes the coat elegant and refined. The base is cotton, fully-embroidered with petit point motifs. I was fascinated by the optical effect of the embroidery, dense and minute, which seen from a distance is transformed into a play of subtle colours that fuse into a whole. CONSUELO CASTIGLIONI, MARNI

Marni, s/s 2004

Haute, haute couture s/s 2004

41

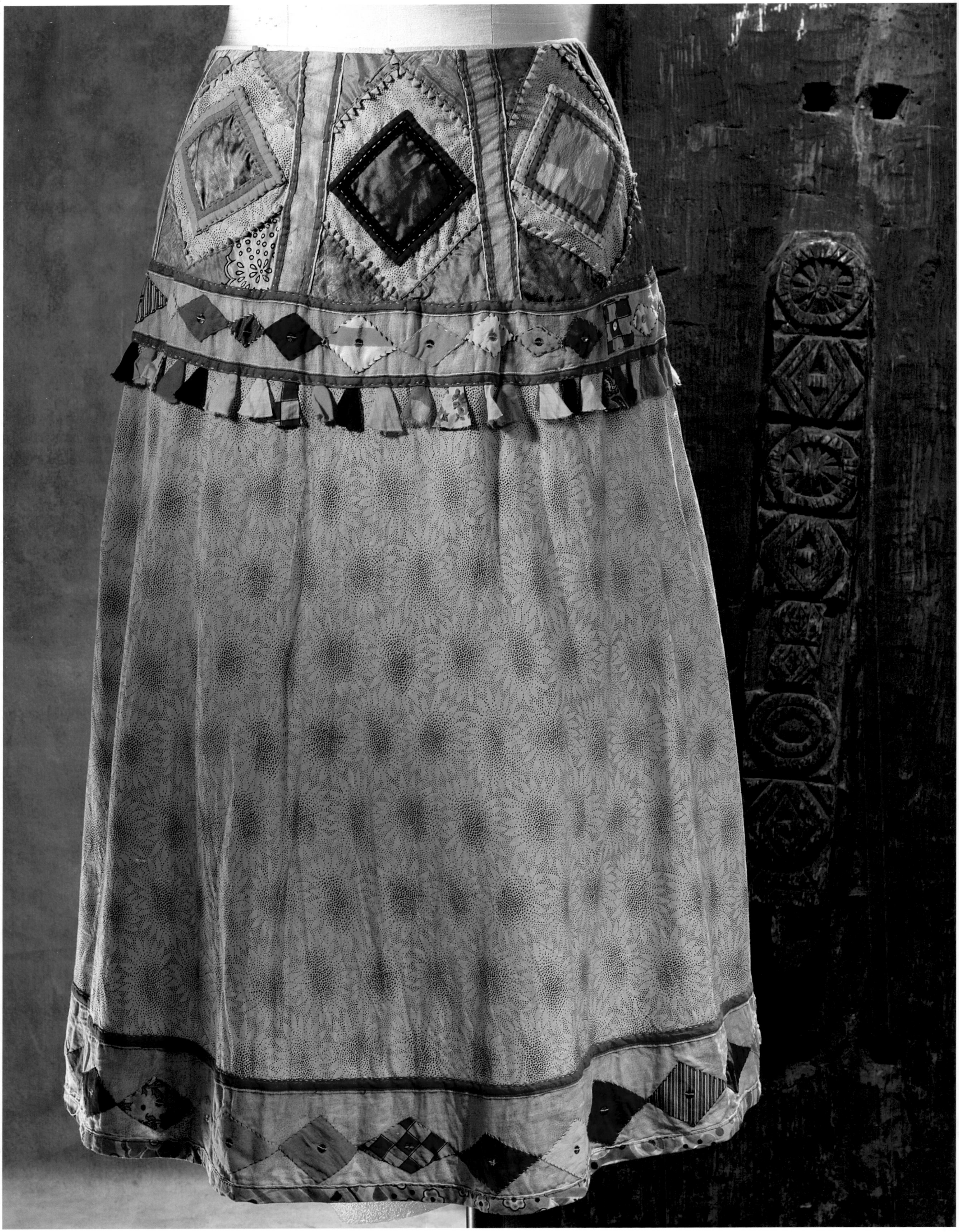

Amen, s/s 2004

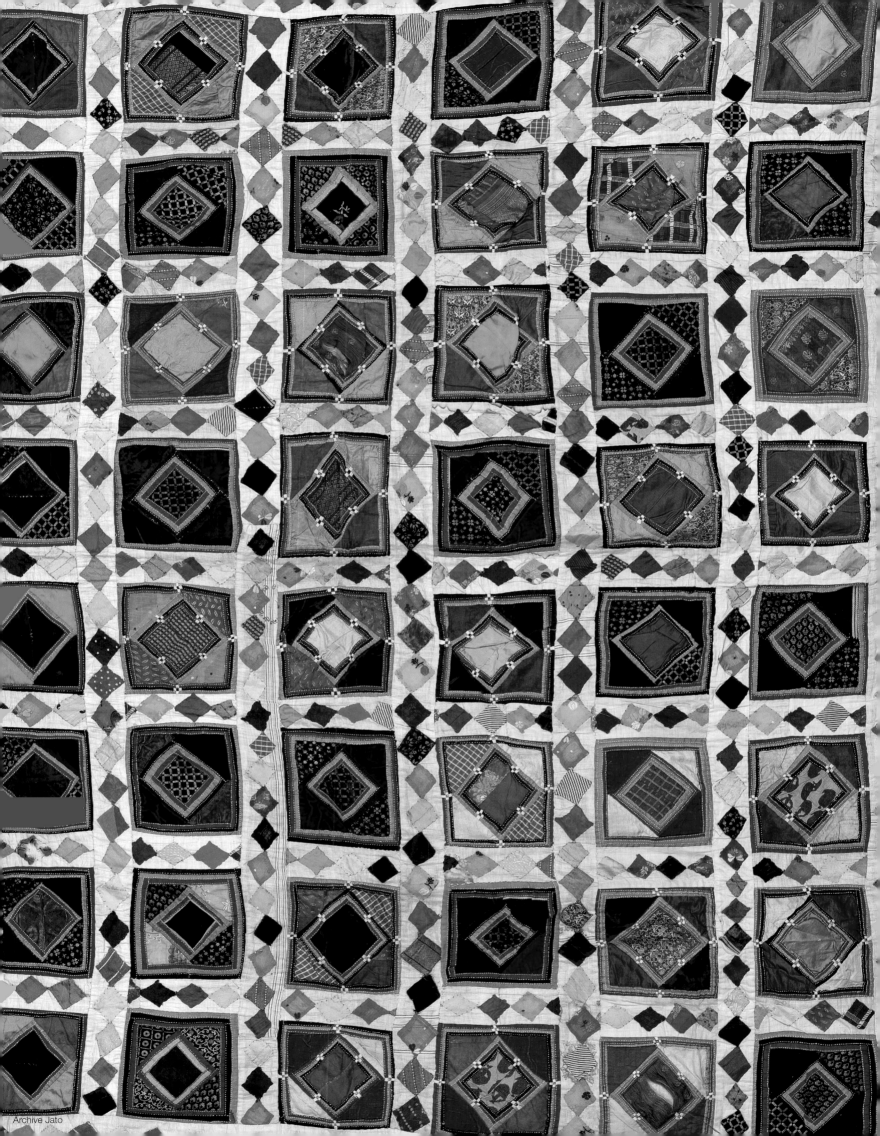

Archive Jato

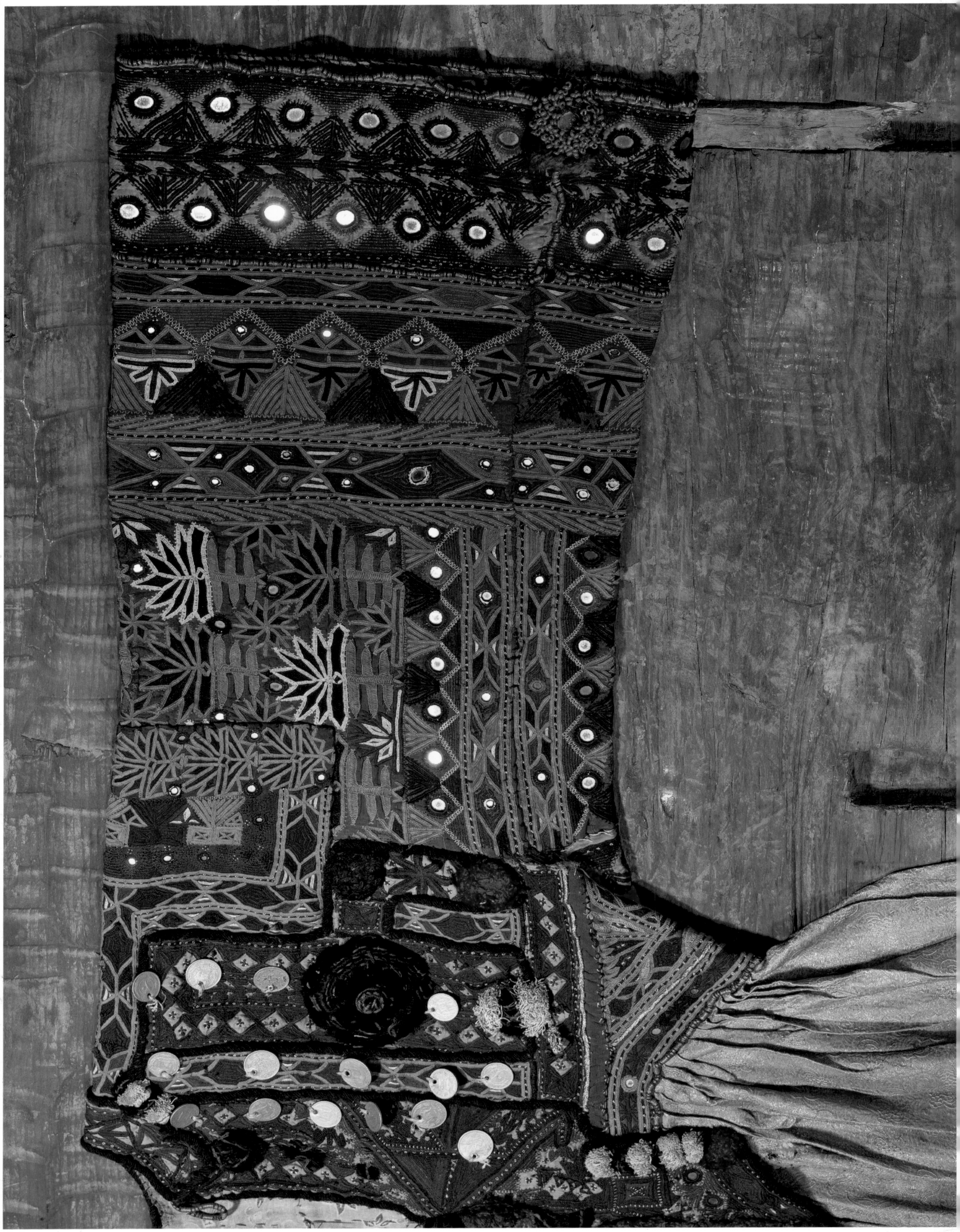

I'm crazy about all ancient traditions because when they're recovered and brought into a modern context they become absolutely topical. Many say that old techniques, for a long series of reasons, cannot be used nowadays.

But I believe that if you really want to use those techniques you can overcome any obstacle and difficulty. The industrialised work process, also in fashion, may be a help and not merely a hindrance in preservation of the oldest techniques of embroidery and decoration in general. Dresses for the show can also be handmade, with great expending of time, means and work, and indeed we very often create items for the show in a more or less bespoke manner.

Then, in production, the same items are made in the industrialised version. Which is not necessarily an evil, because sometimes the limitations that industrial creation constitutionally imposes may also be stimuli that give some extra touch to the garments.

I adore traditions, perhaps because I'm the son of emigrants, perhaps because I'm half English, born and brought up in Great Britain, but I'm also half Italian. And I must admit to greatly identifying with the typically romantic Italian side. I especially identify with Sicilian tradition as it came down to me from my parents… which perhaps doesn't correspond to reality but certainly to the idealisation of it that my memory and imagination have created.

In my approach to fashion I always try to develop something I have in my heart. Even if it's something I've never experienced, something I've only been told about or have imagined. ANTONIO BERARDI

I'm a bit like a magpie. I like everything that glints. Mirrors in particular fascinate me tremendously. I adore mirrors though I don't at all like seeing my reflection. In my opinion the things reflected in mirrors somehow remain magically imprisoned in them. Mirrors contain all the images, thoughts and feelings that have passed before them. Although you can never see them again, you know that the shadows of the passage of all the people who have been reflected are in there and will remain forever. This, I feel, makes mirrors fascinating but also scary: where mirrors are concerned I experience almost reverence, if not actually fear. ANTONIO BERARDI

Embroidery is part of the Emilio Pucci tradition inasmuch as my father took inspiration from Renaissance paintings to embellish the dresses he designed. He was particularly inspired by beads and semiprecious stones. My father began with the designs of his prints and then enriched and beautified them with various types of stones, Swarovski crystals, paillettes, jet, bugle beads and other things in his special colours set out on the dress, following the lines of his prints. This tradition and taste is still the Emilio Pucci style today.

I see embroidery as being synonymous with great dexterity, with research and certainly with luxury and elegance, but also with creativity and highly skilled craftwork. Embroidery will generate emotion in the beholder and wearer only when there is coherent synergy between creative refinement – expressed in the use of interesting lines and fascinating materials – and a technical expertise that ranges through the most special and precious work processes. And embroidery achieves this aim of striking the emotions especially when – as in the case of Emilio Pucci embroideries – it succeeds in being embroidery that is precious in every sense. LAUDOMIA PUCCI

For the embroidery of this skirt we set out, as often happens, from an antique example. A 19th century piece to be exact, practically destroyed, bought at a street market. What we liked most about it was a small detail: the embroidery resulting from the composition of cut out holes with tiny circles of velvet cut out and applied. It was an extraordinary work. We bought it and had it redone. It's fairly rare for me to take a vintage piece and have it faithfully and slavishly reproduced. But in this case I gave in to the charm of the detail. But of the detail I "copied" only the embroidery typology, the technique. As for the lines, the design and all the rest, I preferred to completely reinterpret and reinvent the piece. MAURIZIO PECORARO

Maurizio Pecoraro, s/s 2002

Or you can wear a cotton blouse with embellishments, preciousness, and that's quite another thing. Women know this perfectly well, they know themselves and they know fashion, they are aware and well educated, they know the subject "embroidery" very well indeed. They know that arriving at a party with an embroidered dress is quite different from arriving at a party with an unembroidered, I should say almost anonymous dress. Women feel richer wearing a decorated dress.

Embroidery may be synonymous with luxury, may be synonymous with elegance… it depends on how you interpret embroidery and how you do it. It also depends – especially – on who does it. It may be one thing, may be another. In my case I hope it's both things together. I hope it isn't just one or the other. I hope I succeed in uniting luxury and elegance by means of embroidery.

Some of my colleagues are certainly especially sensitive to embroidery. Some are to be admired for their absolute knowledge of the subject. Others unfortunately use embroidery only because they have to, because it's fashionable, it's the trend, so they dive into it headlong. I am happy to mention Alber Elbaz among those who best know embroidery and how to use it. When he uses embroidery Elbaz knows what he's using. When he talks about it he knows what he's talking about. I think he has embroidery right there inside. He's somebody like me. He loves embroidery and he likes getting into it, into the heart of its history. He doesn't just take an embroidery and copy it. He loves to interpret it and make its sources of inspiration his own. I feel very close to him in this. Embroidery offers you enormous expressive possibilities, you can range here and there, where and how you like. You can do everything and then some. The difficult part however is not to get lost but to find your own original path.

I think "reinterpretation" is a key word in my vision of embroidery. It often happens that I find antique pieces to copy and then reinterpret. Of course the final result, also in terms of originality, depends a great deal on your sensitivity as a designer. In my opinion there are many who don't know how to reinterpret. They just take and copy. They know that the period is the Twenties and Thirties, they go to the street market, buy two or three dresses and copy them just as they are. But the most serious thing is that they don't merely copy the type of decoration and embroidery. The serious thing is that they also copy the line and style of the garment. I believe that a vintage embroidery should be rendered modern, contemporary. To copy it is easy, anybody can do it, even if they're not in the trade. I feel we must give something of ourselves to embroideries. When you take a piece of antique embroidery as your inspiration you certainly don't have to change it radically to make it contemporary. That too would be a mistake. You must retain the flavour of the antique piece, respect it, but you must also manage to render it modern in form. Among other things you have to keep in mind that antique pieces cannot, as things stand today, be created in the very same way they were created one or two hundred years ago. The problem is that even if you wanted to you couldn't reproduce those things today. Basically because the manual skill and craft no longer exist. Precisely for this reason I feel it's useless, and not quite right, to copy an antique embroidery without making the effort to render it contemporary, up to the minute. You must make an effort, in seeking a compromise, to do things in a satisfying, dignified way without debasing or destroying the sources of inspiration to which we all inevitably refer. It's a very thin line, and it's easy to fall on either side. You need to know how to achieve and maintain the right balance between reinterpretation and faithfulness to the models of the past.

Embroidering is neither easy nor simple. It's tough. Everybody does it, but it's really difficult to do well, with the right weight and the right lightness. In my opinion, few succeed.

I think embroidery is in itself one of the most timeless things in the world of fashion. There aren't "yes" and "no" years for embroidery. There are women who adore it, just as there are designers who adore it and who will always use it even when fashion goes somewhat against them. That's how it is with me. I won't bite the hand that feeds me just because minimalism is maybe coming back into fashion. I don't care. I love embroidery and always have. Perhaps I'll interpret it in a less aggressive and forceful way, because I know that the years to come may require a more delicate interpretation. But whatever the case may be, embroidery will certainly never disappear from my fashion design or my world. And in the same way I believe – indeed I'm sure – that women will continue to choose and wear it, even when fashion decrees that it isn't the right moment.   MAURIZIO PECORARO

We had the pillow lace for this garment made in Offida. A few collections earlier – the 1998 spring-summer collection to be precise – I had presented another pillow lace dress on which fourteen women of that little town in The Marches had worked for three and a half months. It was an almost epic event. Offida is famous for lace pillow work. I believe the tradition was brought by a Spanish nobleman in the Cinquecento when he went to live there. In the Spain of those days it was a job done exclusively by men. Today, unfortunately, it is a dying tradition: young people don't want to stay at home working with the lace pillow… The first dress we created was without stitching and was made, as mentioned, by fourteen women, each creating a precise segment as if on a sort of assembly line. Each one created her part, jealously guarding her trade secrets from her colleagues. Two examples of that dress were made: one is now in the Metropolitan Museum of New York and the other in the Offida Museum. It was a really fine job, interesting and fascinating because we also had bone bobbins made, as once used in England. It took us fourtyfive minutes to dress the model for the show: there were buttonholes that had to be closed with bobbins directly on the body of Naomi Campbell.

A few seasons later, the collection this dress belongs to was dedicated to Lucrezia Borgia: it was very dark, Goth, but also punk. The result of the combination of that type of inspiration and old traditional lacework was this dress. The lace pillow technique will shortly disappear, which is a great shame. It's marvellous to see the work being carried out. Because over and above the technical virtuosity, what I like is the emotional charge I personally get from this type of execution. I remember my grandmother doing it when I was small, and it is as if this work process came directly out of my diary and memory. I always try to retain certain emotions, certain moments, certain memories and to put them into my collections. Also with regard to embroidery. Because only in this way can a collection be the total and perfect expression of what I am at a given moment and of what I want to communicate. The choice of lace pillow work was perhaps precisely this: the decision to develop a memory, which is to say an important part of myself. ANTONIO BERARDI

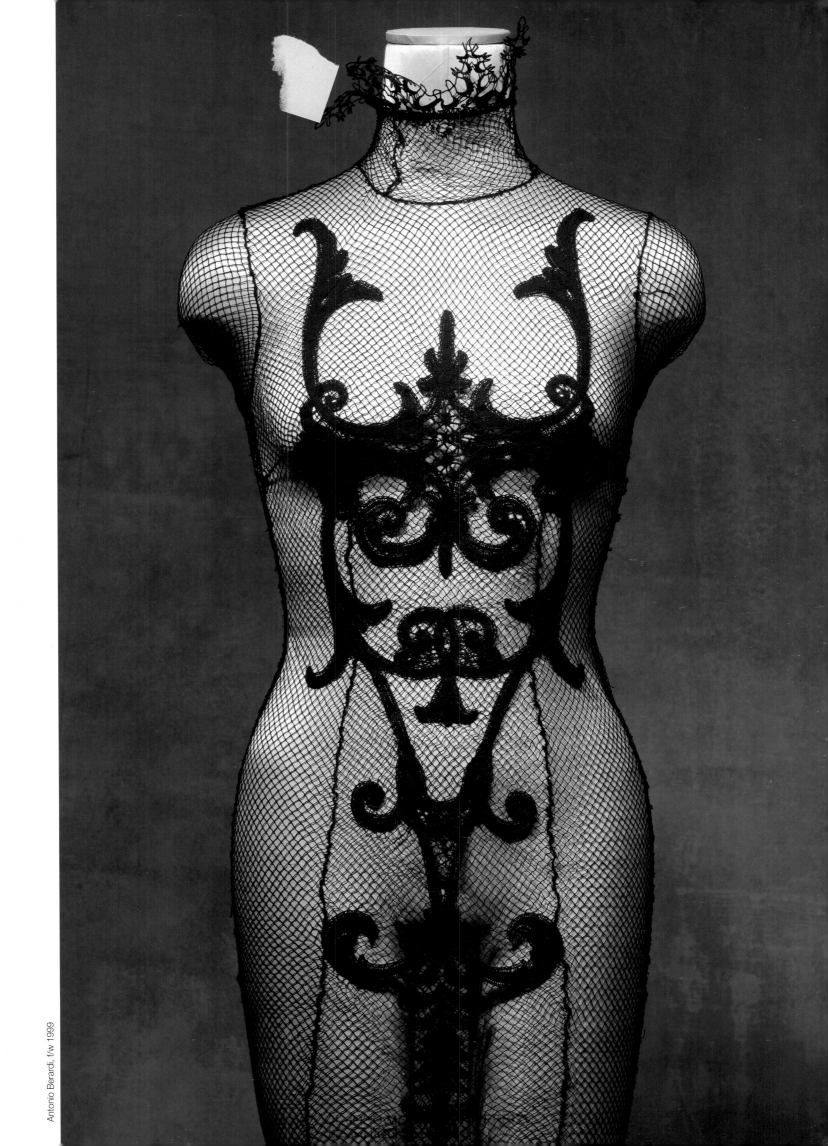

Antonio Berardi, f/w 1999

In drawing inspiration from the past I realise that I invariably choose the same epochs and completely ignore others, skip them.

Basically I like very classic things so, for example, I love the 18th century. I like looking at this period of history and finding inspiration in it, but at the same time I really like contrasts too. So it may happen that I see an 18th century embroidery I like a lot and it immediately triggers a desire to do research on materials, dig up unexpected things to use for a revamping of that embroidery, for example little iron balls… But the procedure is never quite identical. Or: it's always the same but is resolved in a different way each time.

Contrarily I detest and avoid the fashion of the 1980's. The Eighties woman needed to stand out at all costs. She needed to walk into a room and hear a chorus of "Wow!". Today's woman also needs to seduce, and rightly continues to seek an ally in her clothes. But seduction itself has changed and consequently also the way a woman "decorates" herself because – I feel – that this too was influenced by minimalism. I wouldn't venture to say that the period we're living in is exactly low profile, but as far as I'm concerned the search for understatement is decidedly and increasingly important; or at any rate the wish to be as special as possible. I believe that self-decoration now has a meaning rather of being unique, whereas in the Eighties it meant stepping into line.

The priority I give to materials like lace and macramé, for example, certainly comes under the heading of a less flamboyant choice of decoration, softer and less "brilliant". ROSSELLA TARABINI for ANNA MOLINARI

It looks like Russian embroidery but actually originated from a border, worked à filet and then embroidered, which was set around a bed. This border was usually white and was applied to the wedding night bed. I like to tell about the distant inspirations that are elaborated and transformed into embroidery. Whether they be shells from the sea, my mother's old coral necklace or my grandmother's shoe, the only thing of hers I kept. ANTONIO MARRAS

Embroidery as romantic element. I wanted a sensation of the cheerful and carefree in the two-colour effect embroidery – white background and red thread – and in the floral motifs.   CONSUELO CASTIGLIONI for MARNI

Embroidery is enormously important in Valentino fashion design. It's one of the essential elements of dressmaking, of its history and of the dexterity linked to my work. Asking me about the importance of embroidery is like asking a painter about the importance of oil colours.

As regards my style, embroidery is plot, substance, story and technique, but it is also decoration, frieze and ornament. It can give breadth and depth to the simplest garments. It can evoke a story that passes through all ages and civilisations. It's no accident that embroidery, the decorative development of sewing, is found in most refined and advanced cultures.

Like all traditional manual techniques embroidery lives on the past and the future. The most fascinating thing about embroidery is embroiderers themselves. The idea that there have always been and still are women dedicated to it. Like the Venetian embroiderers. I only hope that there are couturiers who will continue to work with them.

Manual skill magically unites human beings. It's one of those unexplainable things without which life would not be the marvel that it is. Try looking at and touching one of my embroideries or those of a great Japanese craftsman and tell me if you aren't moved. If not, think of who did it, what it represents for his sensuality. I think that embroidery gives personality to anything whatsoever. VALENTINO

My sources of inspiration were natural forms and elements. Raw textiles, highly charged greens and earth tones. Embroidery on jute perfectly recalled the irregular lines of nature, randomness and at the same time its perfect harmony. CONSUELO CASTIGLIONI for MARNI

I feel the 80's was the least attractive period in the history of fashion. I never liked the style and I've never revamped it. Those were over-the-top years and fashion proposed – indeed imposed – exaggeration of proportions, colours, forms and even the use of embroidery which in my opinion touched on the ridiculous. Women were crushed by that idea of fashion and by the style of decoration it involved.

I prefer today's fashion and the greater delicacy it expresses, also in the use of embroidery. A thoroughly modern girl can now dress in a pair of jeans, quilted military jacket, a pair of boots and a top with a little rose embroidered at the cuff, as if to say: "OK, I'm a modern girl, dressed in strict accordance with the regulations of fashion, but I'm still feminine!". I love the kind of woman who knows how to dress that way, with that style. I really love femininity and romanticism. I think, and I'm firmly convinced, that with what's happening around us nowadays, everything we see in the world and in fashion, there should always be a background of seduction, romanticism and *broderie*.   ANNA MOLINARI for BLUMARINE

Blumarine, s/s 2004

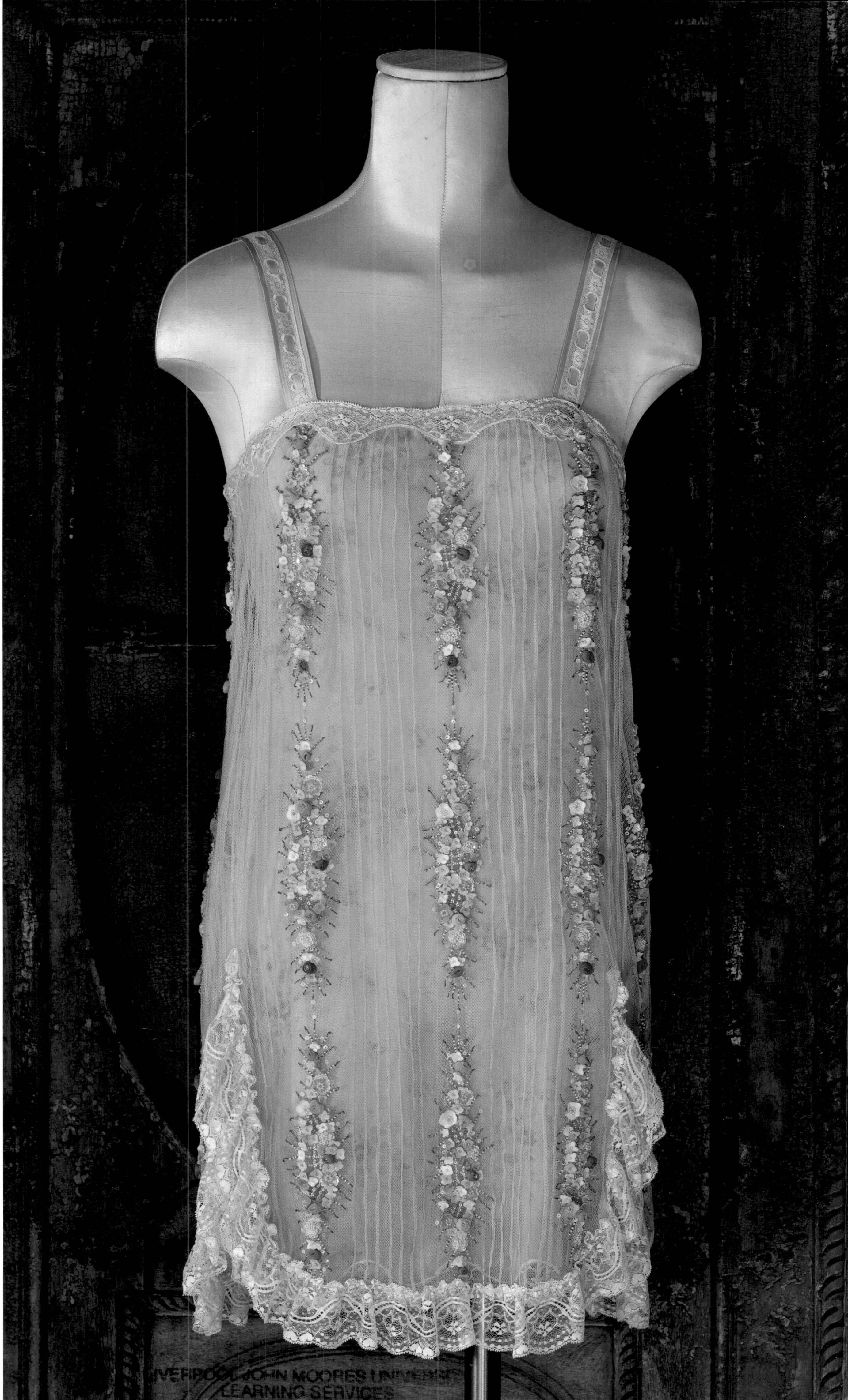

I've loved embroidery since I was little because my mum used to embroider my dresses, my jerseys and underskirts. She was very romantic in the taste she expressed in dressing me. I got my love of embroidery from her and cultivated it over the years, always going to street markets in search of antique embroidery and reading about the history of embroidery...

What interests me in a piece of embroidery is the technical aspect, the material aspect and the design. Looking for new materials is always interesting and I'll never stop doing it. If I see a material I've never used, such as a marvellous Swarovski crystal with a thousand facets, or beads that look antique or a silk that gives the impression of a real flower, I immediately feel the desire to experiment and see what might come of it.

In the same way I pay great attention to the technical side of creating embroidery, because without continual renewal of techniques there is no true research.

Of course the process of study for the design and placing of a piece of embroidery greatly intrigues me. I love looking at the lines used in the past, in ages whose canons of beauty and harmony are closest to my own. I study and analyse them and then reinterpret them in accordance with my personal taste. ANNA MOLINARI for BLUMARINE

I very often start out with an idea of embroidery and build a dress around it. Without embroidery my dresses are incomplete. For my creations embroidery is essential in the most literal sense of the word. The fabrics I look for or the cuts I experiment with always involve the idea of embellishing them afterwards with an embroidery story. I never imagine evening gowns in velvet or satin completely without embroidery or applications… I always imagine them by setting out from beautiful basic fabrics which however cry out for embroidery. An evening gown is not for the evening, in my opinion, if it isn't embroidered. I often like a woman to be dressed exclusively in, precisely, embroidery. It changes little if the embroidery is all over or only involves certain specific details of the garment. The important thing is that embroidery should be there. It's something that comes from my DNA. I couldn't make a dress without embroidery. And this idea isn't limited to evening wear but also includes knitwear, dresses in more masculine fabrics and shapes, jeans, quilted winter jackets and even accessories, shoes and bags. Everything that is embroidery makes my creations softer and highly recognisable. Only embroidery can make a garment special and unique. I use embroidery in everything, but always softly, very gently and prettily. In fact they called me the "queen of roses". Because I really love this flower and I put it everywhere, but with discretion, delicately, so it is never oppressive. ANNA MOLINARI for BLUMARINE

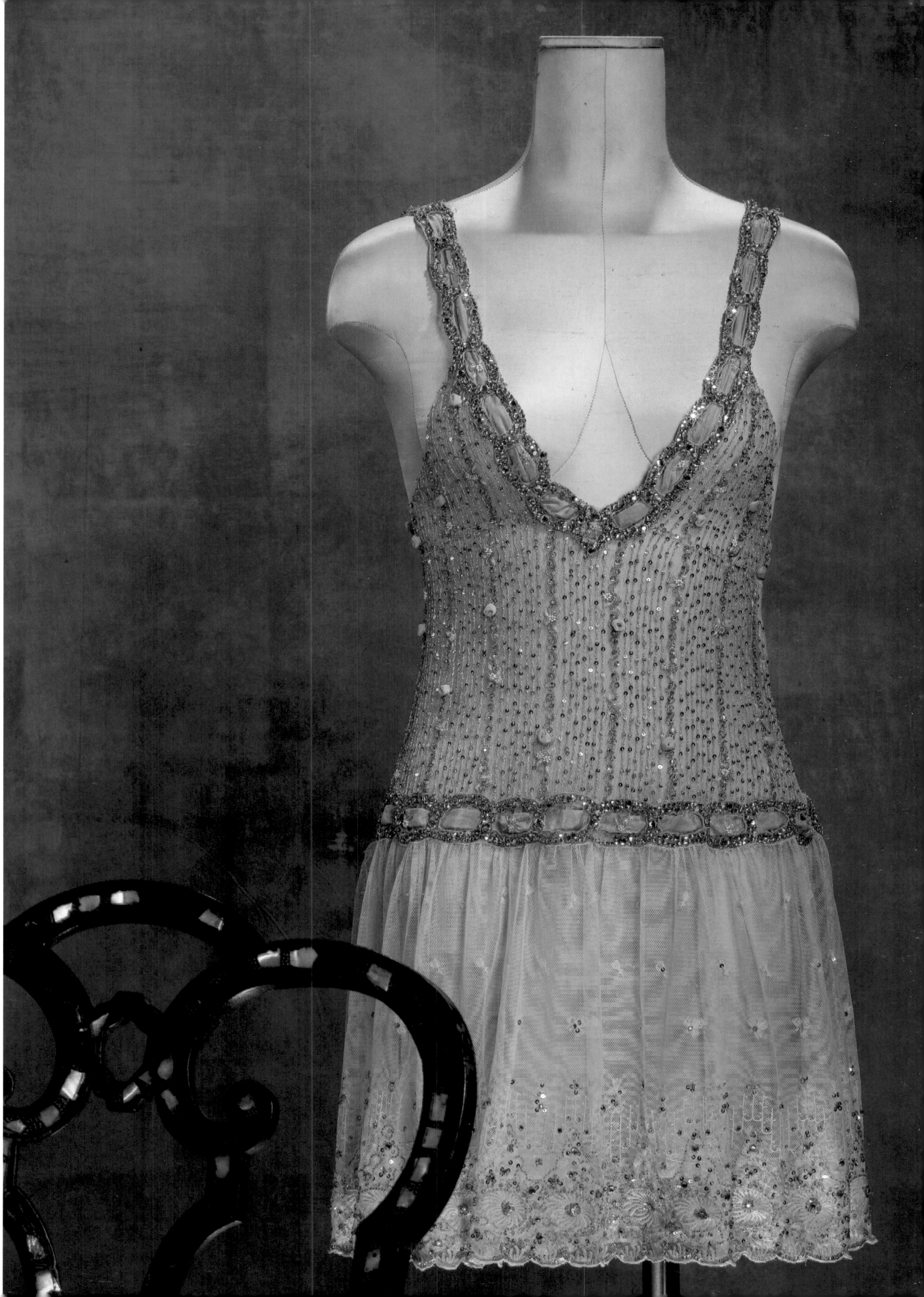

Blumarine, s/s 2004

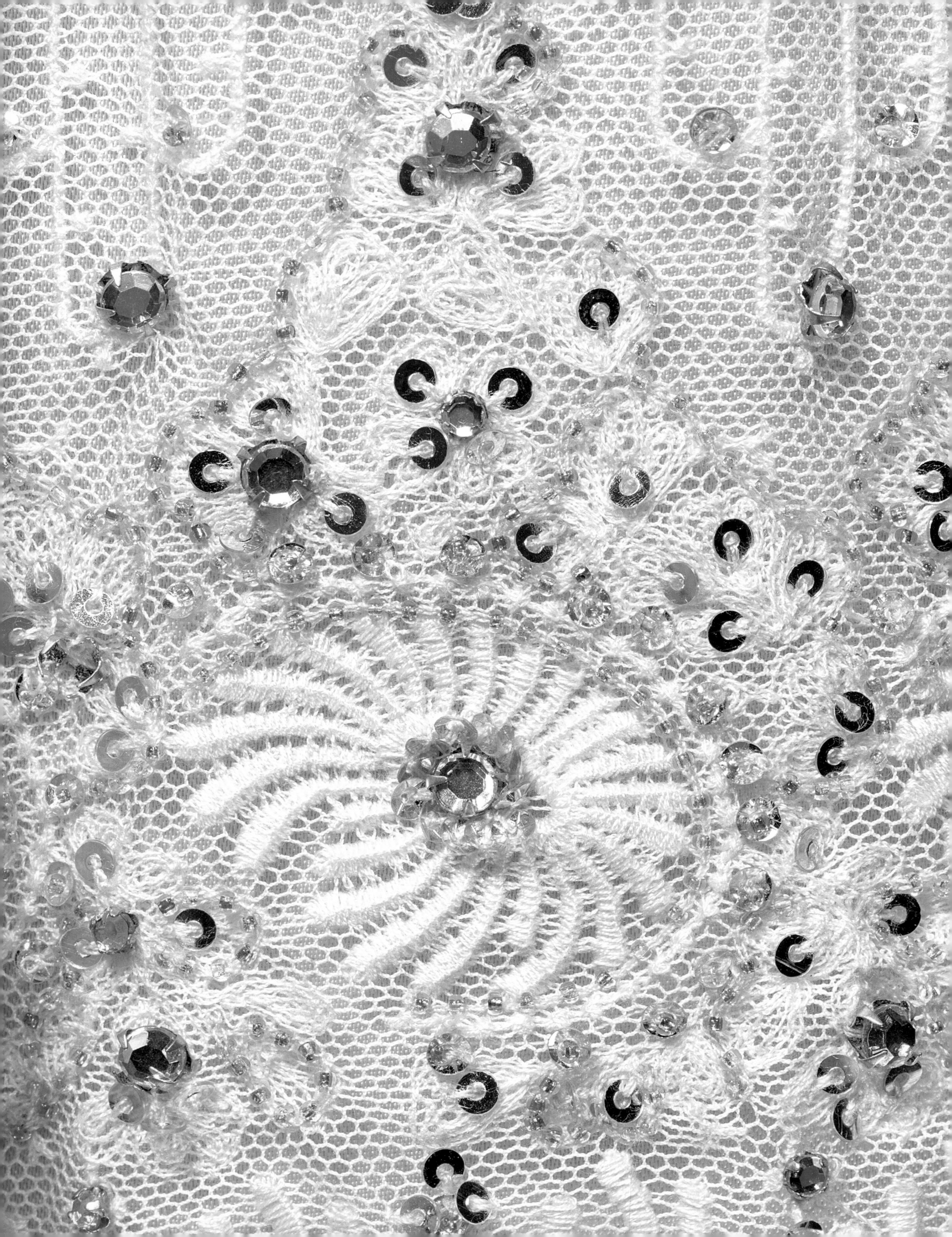

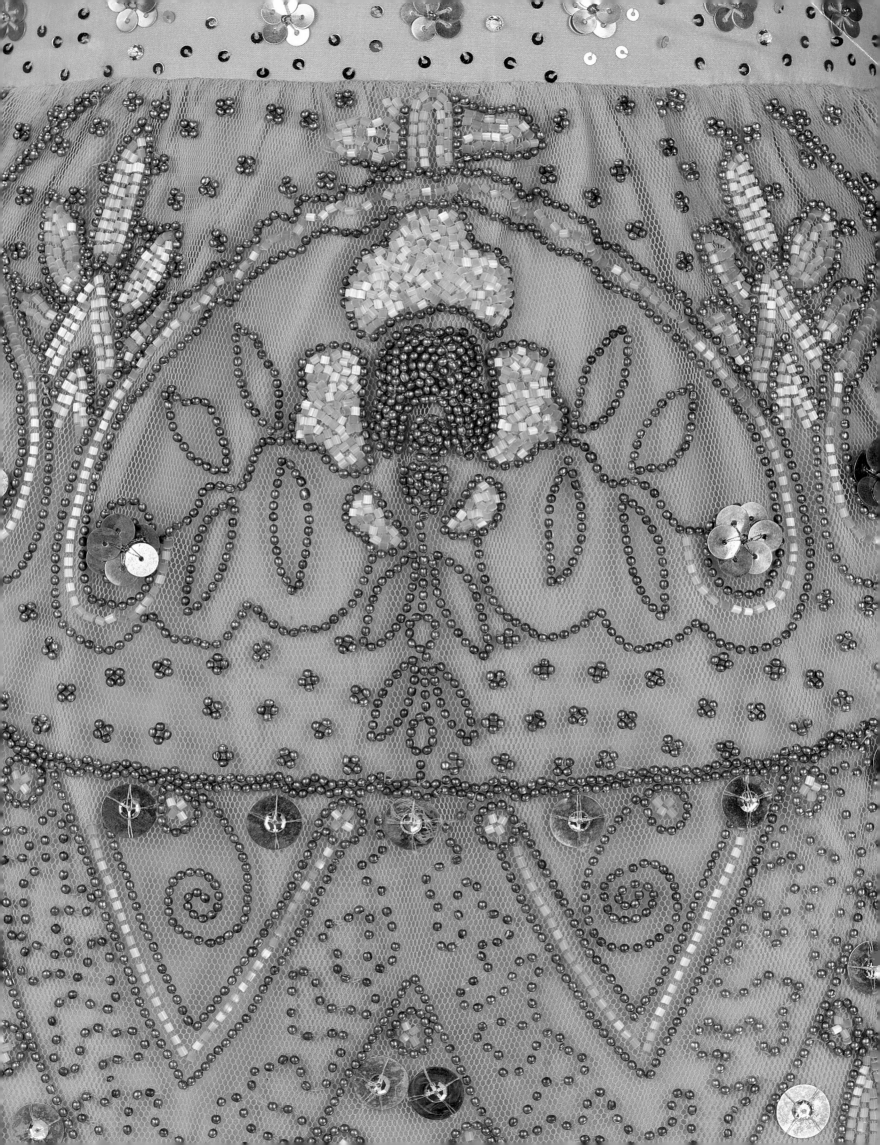

Blumarine, f/w 2000

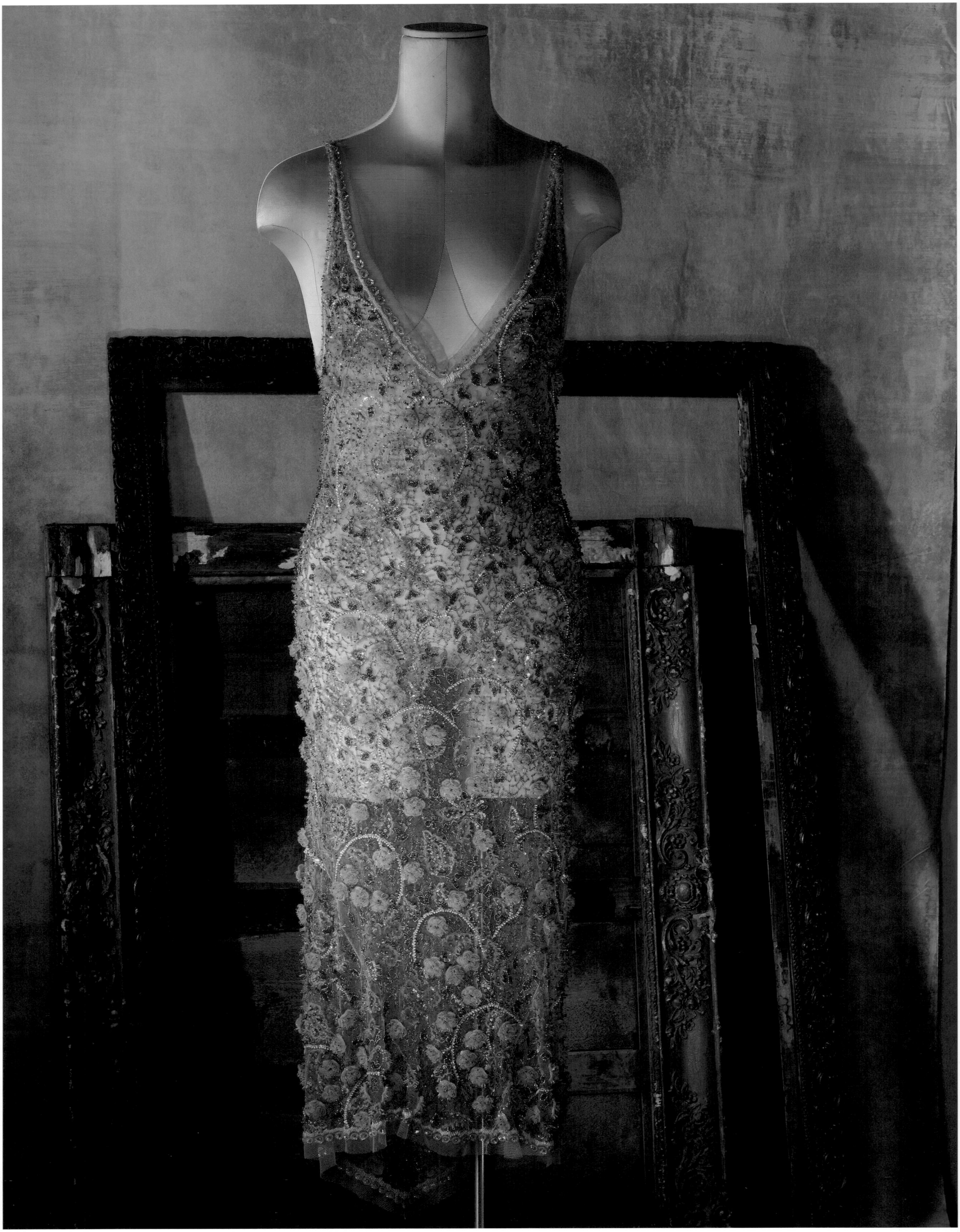

To people who ask me what I think about the fact that some are starting to talk of a return to order and rigour – after the maximalist emphasis of the past decade – I can only reply that there's always somebody saying that something will end and something else begin. Actually there have been very few real changes since the female silhouette slimmed down. And very few of us took part in these moments. Fashion is like all other forms of creativity. Epoch making changes need epochs, not semesters. VALENTINO

Valentino, haute couture f/w 2002

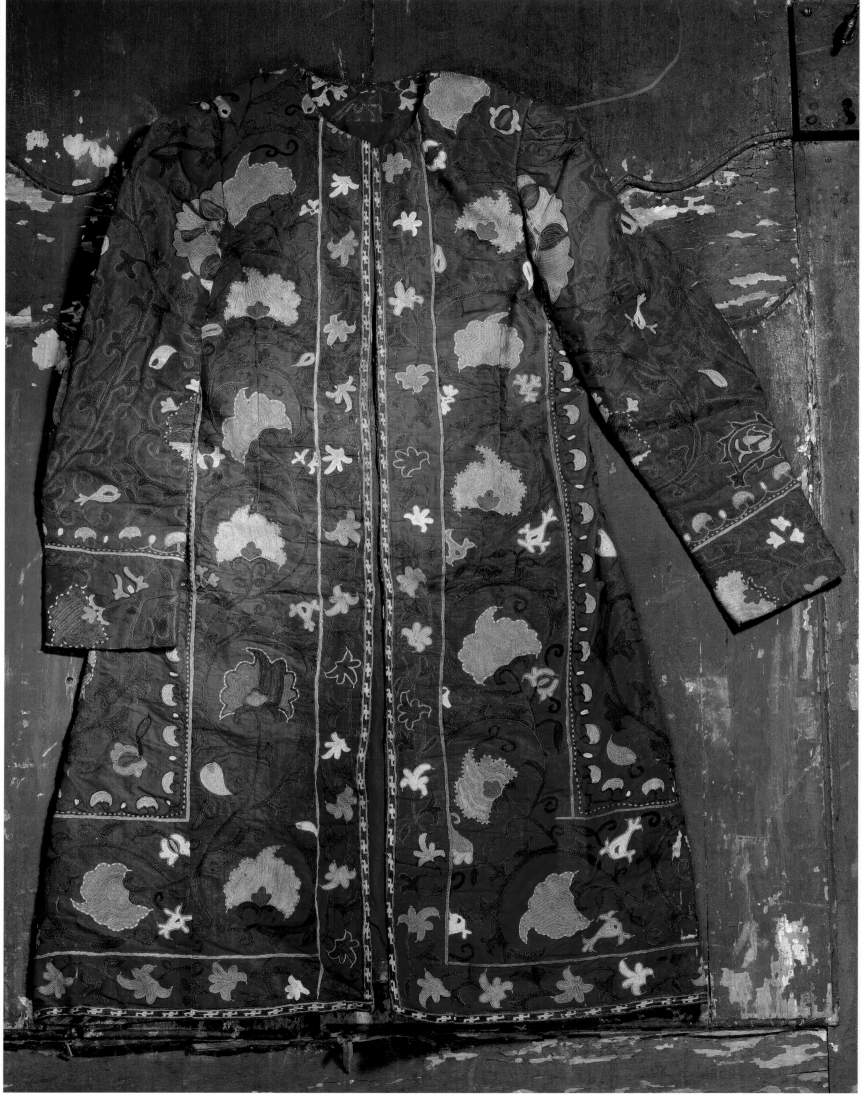

Amen, s/s 2005

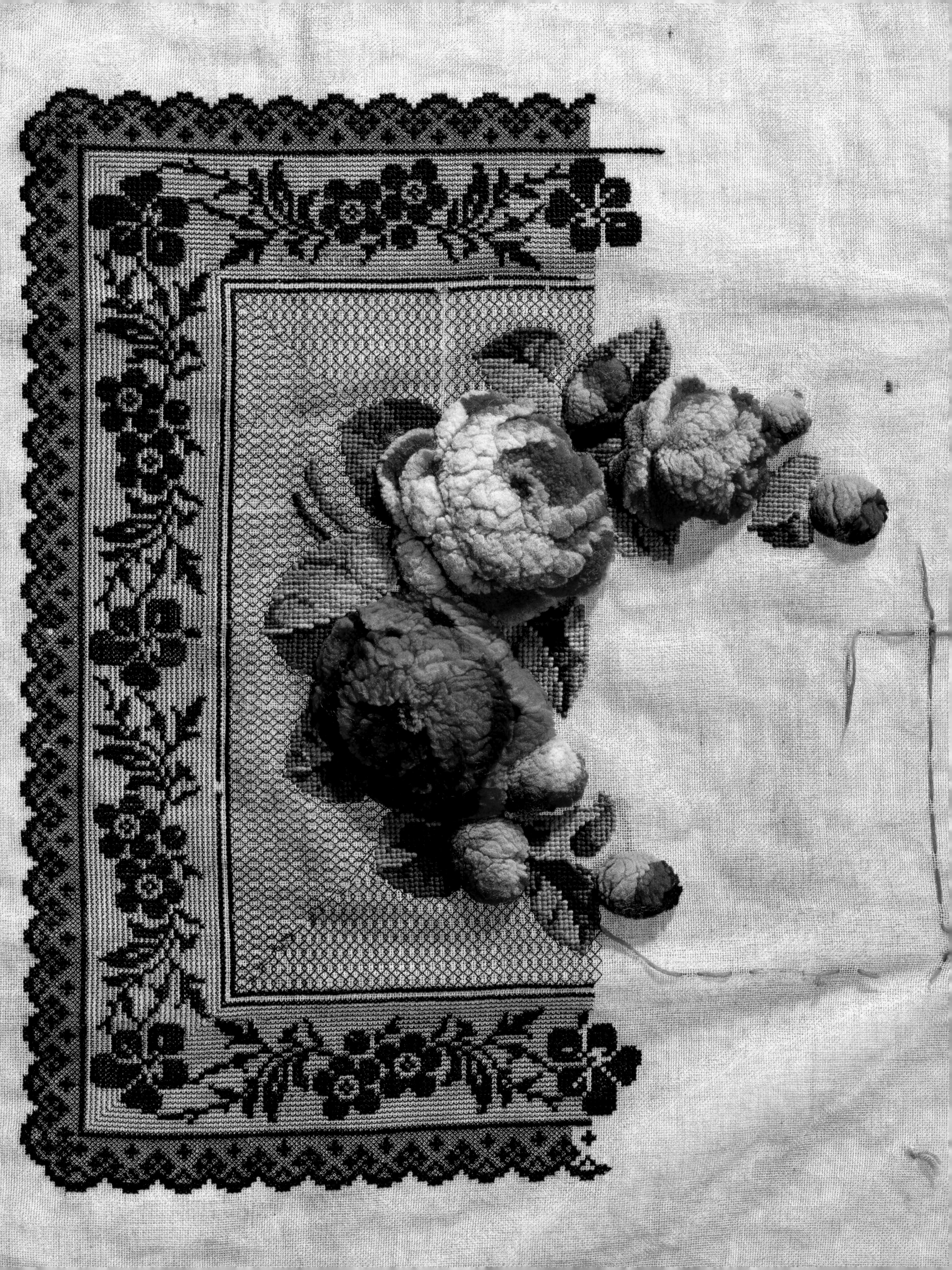

Archive Jato

Any inspirational departure point is valid for my creations. I set out from a jacket, a pair of trousers, a theme or a material… but what interests me in all cases are the passages, the layers, the elaborations that may occur with regard to my initial object as I modify, transform and refine it. The same goes for fabrics. Although I start out with elaborate customised cloths which (it depends) make my manufacturers crazy or joyous – with me they can experiment as much as they like – what I like doing in any case is to intervene on the material. It isn't enough for me to have fabrics ready and waiting. I like to wash them, dye them, assemble them, discolour them, erase them, stain them, deconstruct them.

This is how Sardinian dresses are, absolutely layered and in no way simple, enriched by a thousand interventions. The Sardinian woman typically wears an underskirt with a kind of apron over it and then a skirt… the Sardinian costume is made up of superimposed layers, one upon the other. This is what I like doing in dress design. I like to add something to another thing, and then again another… I'm often accused of putting "too much" into my creations, and the fear is that people may not immediately understand them. But my answer is that there's nothing more awful than boredom, and one of my primary needs is to get away from what is boring and taken for granted. And that what is really important to me is to succeed in creating things which correspond one hundred percent to what I seek, things which among a thousand others may be recognised as Antonio Marras creations. And it's not a simple question of needing to stand out. What impels me, what is necessary to me, is the expression of emotions, and this is how I manage to do it. There are many possible ways, but this is mine.

Another thing that absolutely interests me is contrast. I like the challenge of putting together things that are apparently irreconcilable. I like doing what couldn't be done, what seemed impossible to achieve. Assemble, cut, insert… I like to challenge the ostensible laws of harmony. I like enriching something that may appear perfectly harmonious with a dissonant detail that creates a surprising effect. There lies the difference. Clearly this type of work, which calls for repeated manual intervention, requires a high level of technical skill and craftwork. As a consequence only a limited number of articles can be produced. When an individual garment must undergo seven different work procedures and is handled for five days, enormous quantities obviously cannot be produced. For certain things industrial production is unthinkable.

This is the atelier, the workshop where many people do their utmost to achieve what might appear impossible. A continuous job of experimentation, trial, attempt. ANTONIO MARRAS

Ideas come in all kinds of ways, also from things from which you'd never have expected anything. And all things may be the detail or centre of a story. Sometimes an embroidery suggests a garment. Sometimes a garment claims its embroidery. Unlike wanting and knowing how to do things, creation has no rules.   VALENTINO

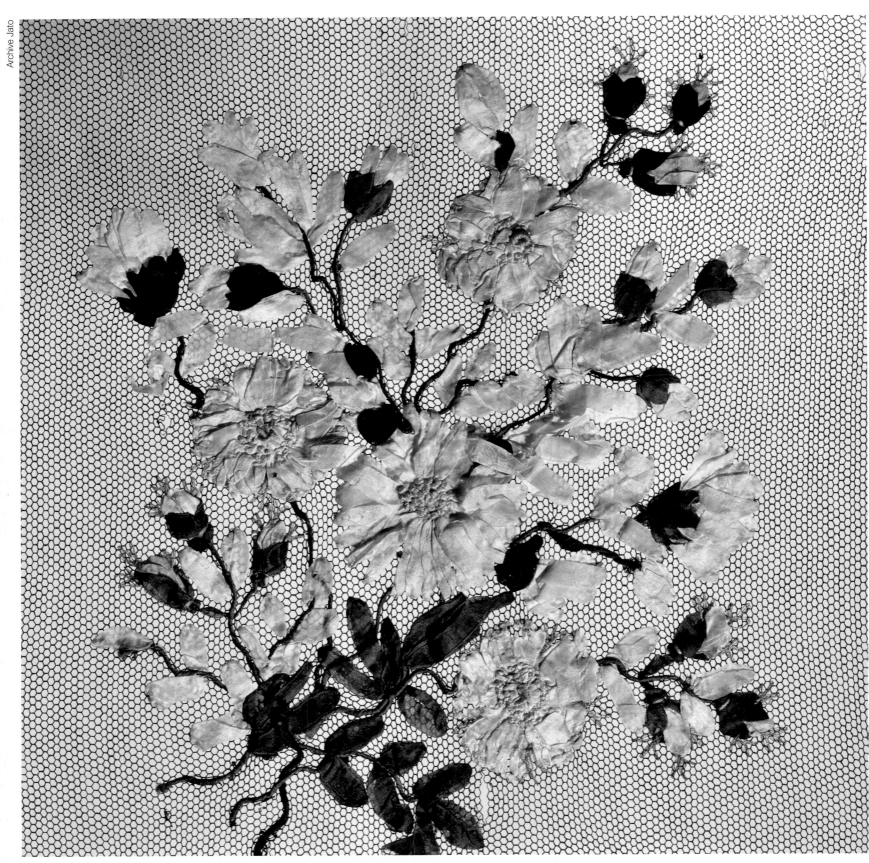

I've seen very simple yet highly elegant embroidery, just as I've seen prodigious embroidery that left me indifferent. And I've also seen fine embroidery done by people who had just begun to embroider. Passion is all.

VALENTINO

Antonio Marras, s/s 2004

Archive Jato

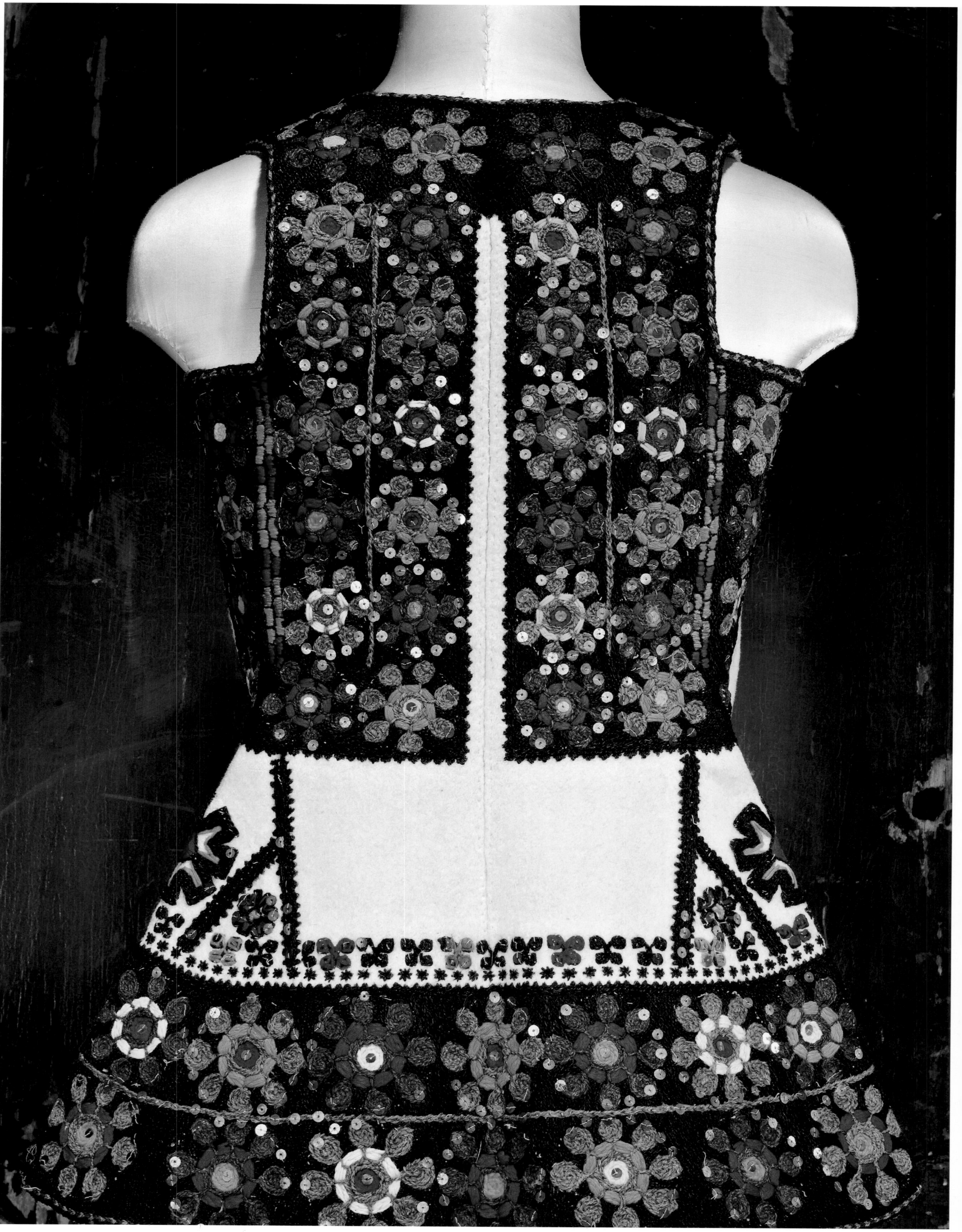

The inspiration was China. The women in this collection seemed to have walked out of a chic Far East bordello. The atmosphere is faked trash; the visual impact of the garments is very powerful yet absolutely not vulgar. In the case of this top, the thread embroidery on tulle appears almost suspended. The skirt in the same series was worn over knitwear culottes. This "now you see it / now you don't" concept of superimposing has become a must with Alessandro Dell'Acqua. The collection featured a stylistic cipher we still retain, which has entered fully into the collective imagination of what the Alessandro Dell'Acqua brand represents today.

We often find inspiration in antique examples of the European embroidery tradition and update them. Technically, the flower on this top could be an antique embroidery, but the interesting and new thing is the way in which the antique embroidery has been revamped. It's very important to succeed in adopting an old technique, but it must be made topical through interpretation of modern taste. This is the bulls-eye we have to hit. We have to be able to maintain past history, culture and technique and at the same time optimise them in a contemporary key. Today this is the only way to make the absolute most of embroidery.

I'm more emotionally attached to certain embroideries. This is one of them: it represents the earliest successes, earliest memories, which remain the strongest and most exciting. With these embroideries we were able to investigate the themes that we were most interested in exploring. And then, this way of offering embroidery gave us a direction and a hallmark which, though enriched with new knowledge, we still use and are recognised by today. ALESSANDRO DELL'ACQUA

I feel that embroidery is closely linked to the sense of memory and preservation of the past. This is how I see it, but unfortunately for the new generations embroidery is limited, is resolved simply with a few paillettes and Swarovski crystals. I believe that embroidery should be much more.

In Italian fashion embroidery is often used merely to enrich a garment, as if by adding a few shimmers a garment automatically gains value. Elsewhere, in France, England and America, there's more research, and every season they try to find some new form of decoration or application. I too always try to find new ideas to develop.

In this sense I think the best exponents of embroidery have been those from whom – to judge by their idea of fashion and style – you would never have expected special use of it. I'm thinking of John Galliano, Gaultier, Miuccia Prada… and even earlier of Charles Frederick Worth and Christian Dior…

At the moment though, I think we're all a bit lazy. To adorn yourself in a certain way nowadays means simply and only "I've got". It was a whole different ballgame at the end of the Seventies and in the Eighties when there was mass and intensive use of embellishment in all its possible forms. But in those days the taste for decoration had come from the streets, especially from the young who had started covering their clothes with brooches, pins, writings and necklaces… something that later exploded in a definitely different way when it was taken over by designers. The times are now changing. A dress alone says nothing now. It needs something "overlaid" to express something. It needs to be heavy. Because today the purpose of a dress, and I say unfortunately, is merely to let people know that you "have" and that you "are" Somebody. Decoration is somehow a social indicator. And Italy shows a very petit bourgeois attitude in this context. Today women wear decorated dresses, including the ineptly decorated, almost as if to say: I've got, and I'll let you see everything I've got, even stuck onto my clothes. And it's really a shame because this conception of dressing, and therefore of fashion, has led to three harmful consequences in the embroidery world for people who still use it and use it "heavily". First: the lack of taste in using embroidery. Second: its frequent descent into vulgarity. Third: its inability to acquire an appearance of modernity.

I myself, though I'm very baroque indeed, make efforts in every collection to seek something that is not so obvious. It's really easy to "lay on" things, stones and paillettes, because this makes a garment look richer. It's almost as if people wanted to say: See how I shine! See how much I'm worth! But I feel embroidery deserves quite another kind of respect. ANTONIO BERARDI

I love the cinema and often draw interesting points of inspiration from it. One of my favourite films is Peter Bogdanovich's Paper Moon. In one scene little Tatum O'Neil is wearing her dead mother's kimono and is smoking a cigarette, feeling herself almost a woman but remaining a little doll. That scene inspired this kimono type tweed coat. I love allusion and I often love to refer, in my dresses, to films, works of art and other things. But always in a discreet, veiled, filtered way. Clear and obvious allusion seems useless to me. People can identify it and I don't think they're very fascinated or interested.   ANTONIO BERARDI

Antonio Berardi, f/w 2001

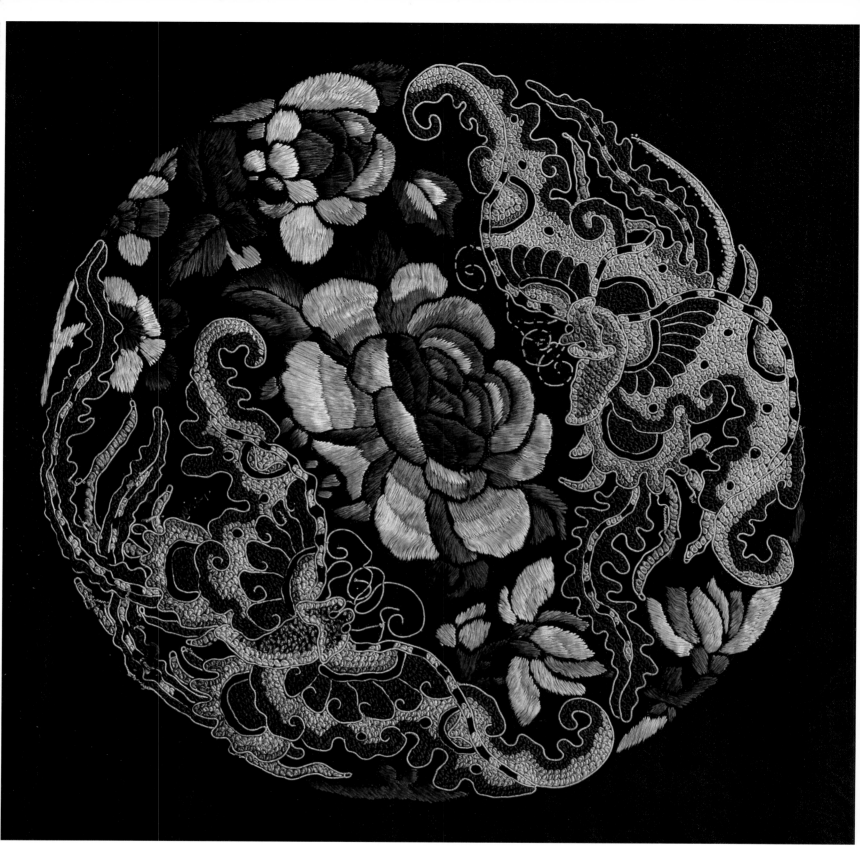

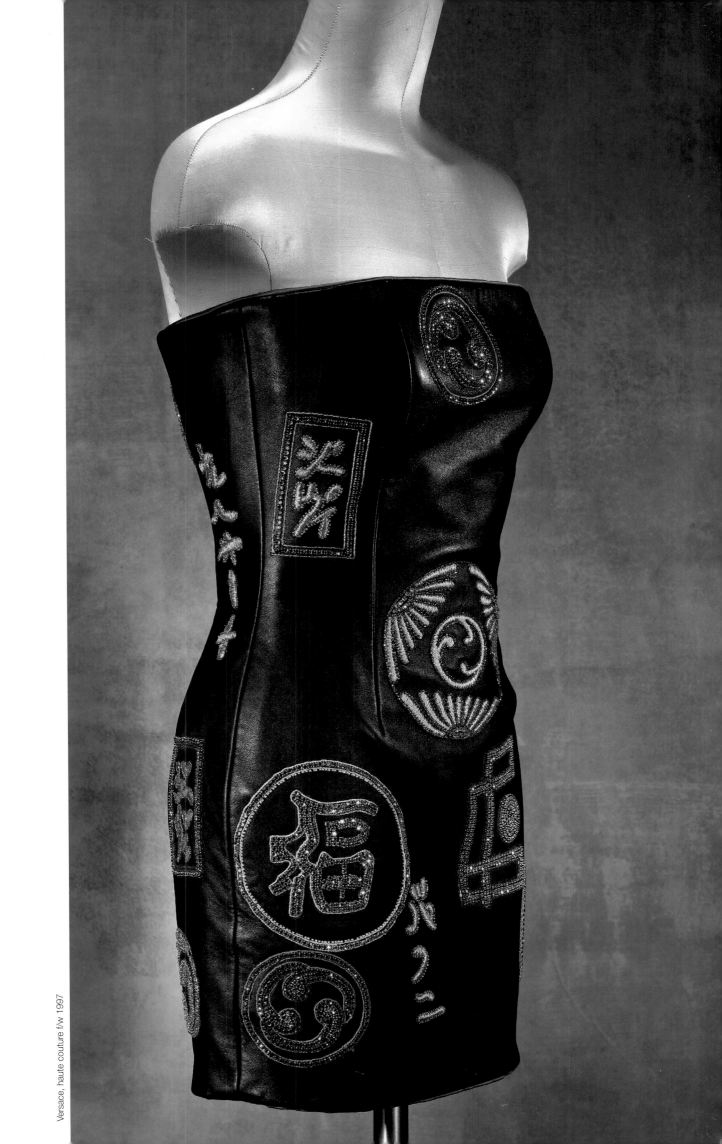

There are no rules for my inspiration: it has a broad range. I don't want to limit it. Absolutely anything might lead to another thing. I'm omnivorous, inquisitive and I always reprove myself for never having enough time to see all the things I'd like to see and have never seen.

An old kimono found in Tokyo, the material of a chair cushion saved from a garbage bin… anything at all may draw my attention, inspire me.

A detail that catches my attention: that's how I like to set out on my work. Especially when the detail is part of a world that I don't know or is distant, that isn't a part of my immediate interests. It intrigues me to go into territories other than my own. ANTONIO MARRAS

I often go to antique markets in search of pieces that might arouse new ideas. I especially like to go when the collection has been completed, to get away from what has been done and clear my head. You get the chance to see what you might do and also learn about what you mustn't do. It's a highly interesting phase of the creative process in which an important role is played both by instinct – which draws your attention to certain stimuli and not others – and by coincidence which exposes you to certain stimuli rather than others.

A collection, and therefore an idea of embroidery, hardly ever springs from a predetermined theme. It almost always sets out from your most instinctive desires, your "animal" curiosity, from what you like at a given moment. It's great to leave the house and let yourself be conditioned and influenced by the bombardment of stimuli that can arrive from the outside world. It's only afterwards, in the reprocessing and reordering phase, that you realise you're on one specific path rather than another. And above all you realise that nothing you absorbed previously was actually random.   VERONICA ETRO

Etro, f/w 2000

All Asian countries fascinate me. I love the far east. In Japan I visited not only Tokyo and Osaka but also Kyoto which is romantic, ancient and very beautiful. I love looking for antique dresses, kimonos, stoles, belts, obis... All marvellous things that give me a vast interior richness, things I go on to reproduce in the form of embroidery for my dresses. I'm a great lover of the beautiful, and for me the beautiful must be something recognisable and universal. The beautiful must be beautiful for everyone, not only for me. I love the beautiful in all its expressions, and I always try to reproduce it in accordance with my personality. ANNA MOLINARI for BLUMARINE

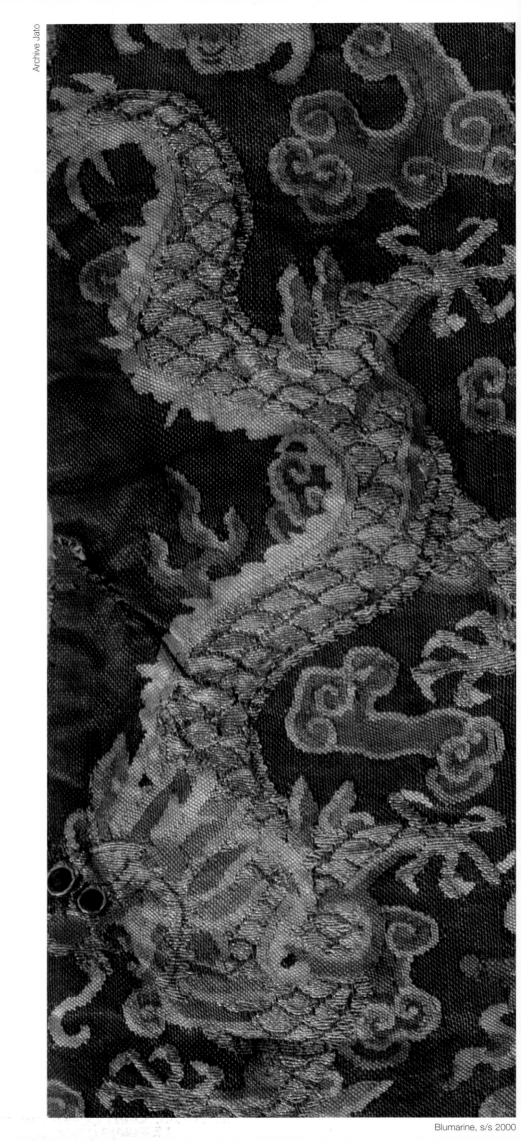

Blumarine, s/s 2000

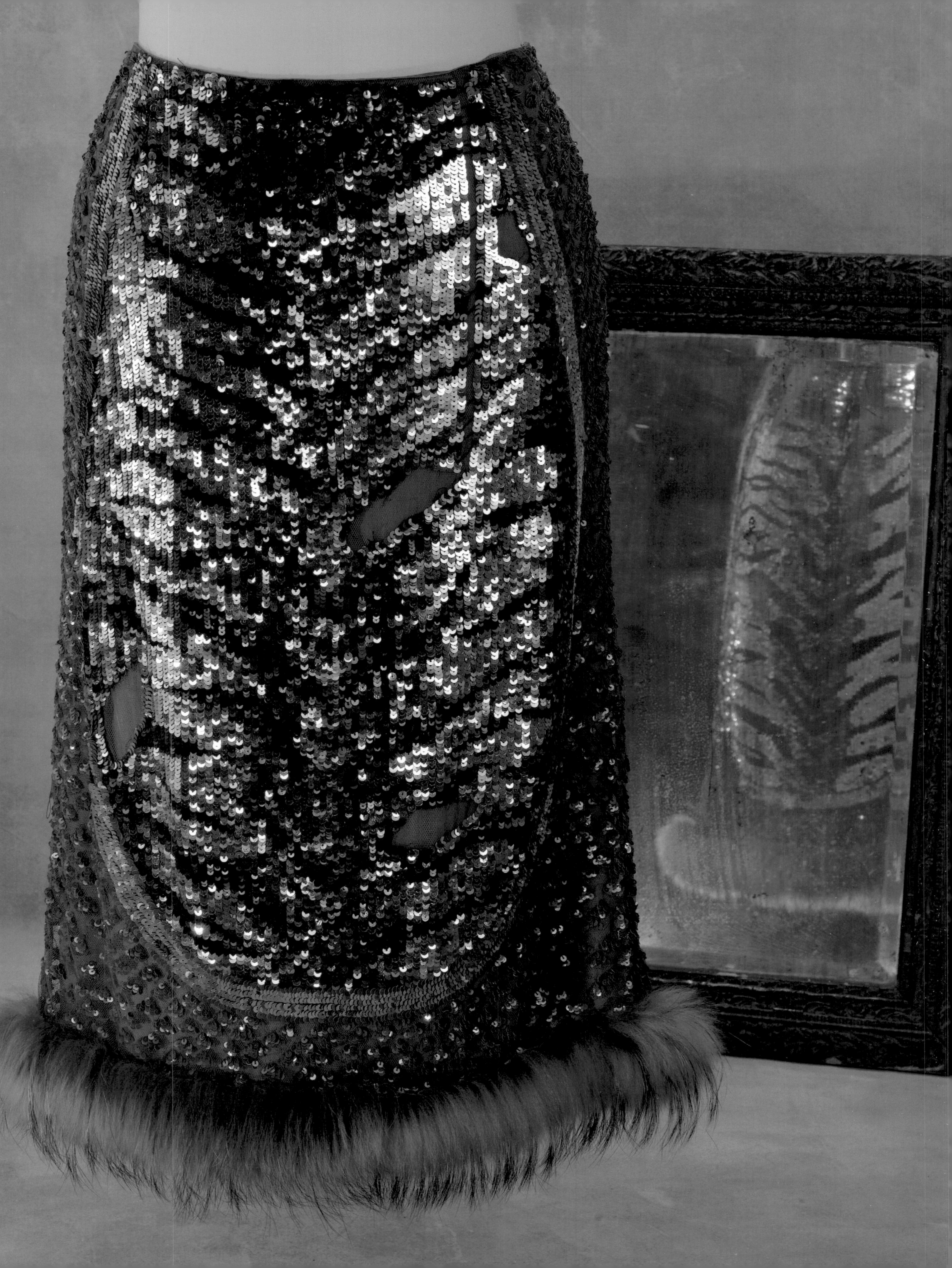

Etro, f/w 2000

What most interested us was experimentation with material. I hope we may say without presumptuousness that we were among the first to experiment with working fur in this way. In subsequent years it was done and done again with increasing frequency. We had some strips of mink cut, with the fur at two different lengths, and then we mixed them with longhair beaver. We mounted these strips in a graphic manner on a tulle base, so that the garment would be versatile and easy to match with other items in the collection. We added turquoises, and this example of an anomalous matching of two very different materials was also pretty innovative: I think it was a great idea to mix something old, like turquoises, with an ancient material – perhaps the most ancient in the history of fashion – interpreted in a new way.   ALESSANDRO DELL'ACQUA

Alessandro Dell'Acqua, f/w 1999

This item grew out of the desire to attempt reverse embroidery of a fur, in this case lapin. It was a challenge. We embroidered the exterior with multicolour Swarovski crystals and leather flowers, and a small part of the internal fur, the visible part, which is to say at the neck. MAURIZIO PECORARO

Maurizio Pecoraro, f/w 2004

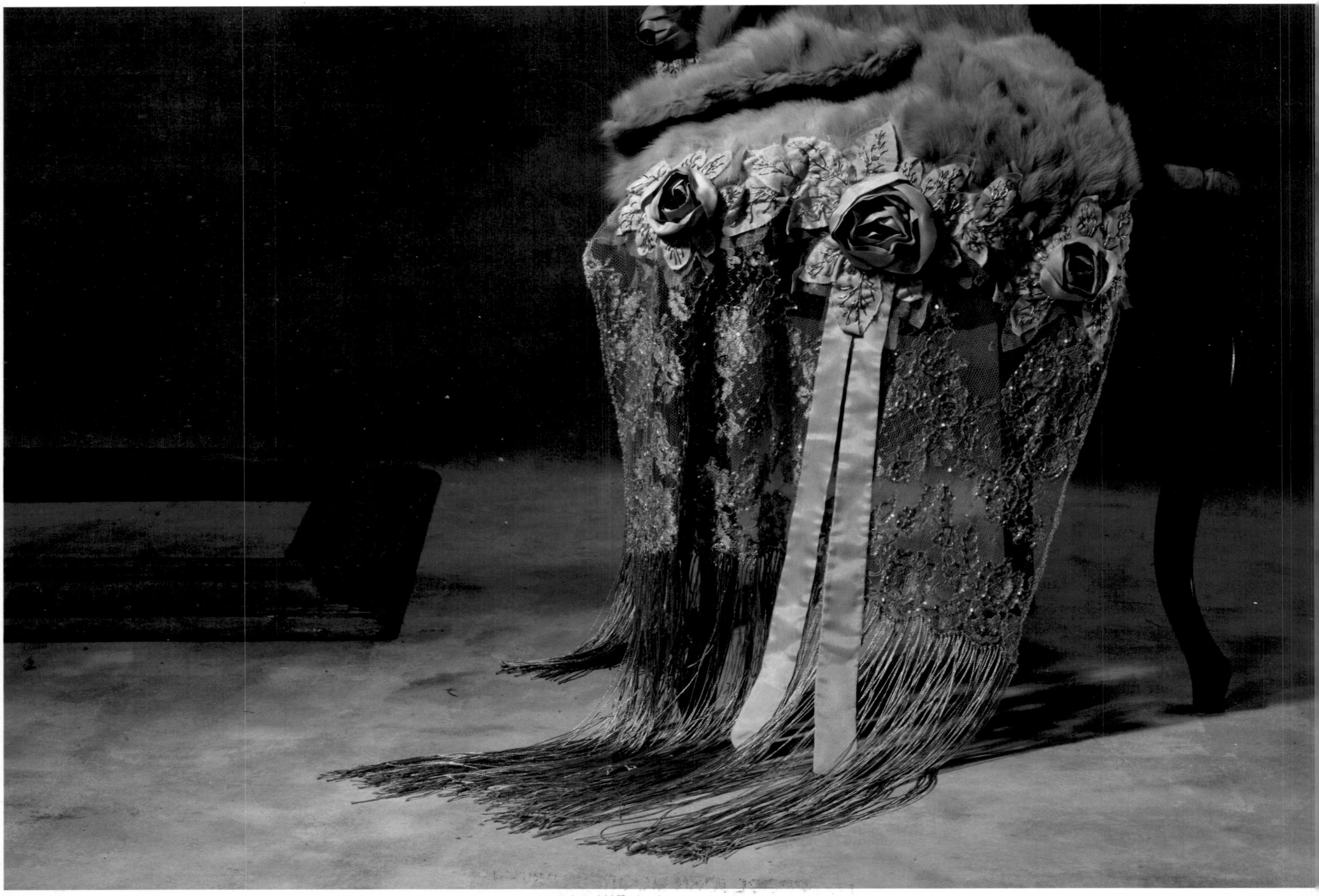

Valentino, f/w 2005

Embroidery is the star of the garment. I was attracted by the play of forms of embroidery done in different materials, superimposed and applied.

Putting together, setting side by side, matching. Creation for me is like making a mosaic of fabrics, prints, styles and finishes which represent a grouping of histories and cultures, places and memories. I try to create dresses that offer exchangeable possibilities and unpredictable effects, collections open to individual choices and sensations.

Embroidery is a technique by which I can transform or embellish a dress and a fabric not only with material but also with meaning. It's like a jewel, a detail that enriches a garment and makes it unique.

In the creative phase its application is subsequent to the study of line and form. It's hard to say what is the most important phase in embroidery development. I draw inspiration from everything around me, creating a "mix and match" in which each element has its own importance. The same goes for the production phases of a fabric or, precisely, of an embroidery. Each moment has its magic that contributes to the whole.

My approach to fashion has always been highly individual. It's timeless and doesn't depend on the trend of the moment. I set out from sensations, the overlaying of stories and styles. This is why I've always preferred a simplicity that allows me to play. The same thing goes for embroidery. I've never followed the dictates of fashion. I select materials, forms and patterns in total freedom, thinking only of the aesthetic balance of the garment I'm working on.   CONSUELO CASTIGLIONI for MARNI

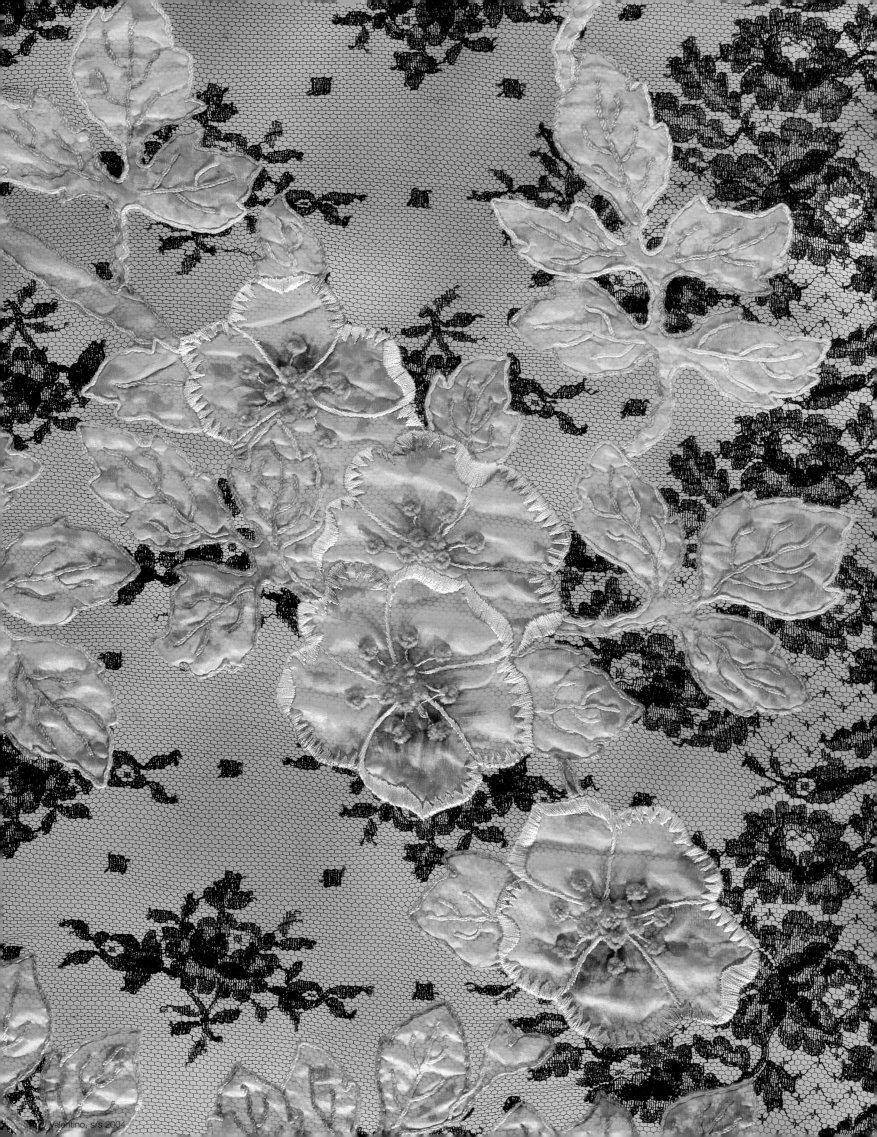

Valentino f/w 2003

I'd like to dissociate the concepts of embroidery and costume which are very often linked. Embroidery may very frequently become costume, or it may become decoration. Whereas for me it is highly important to find a way towards the rebirth of an object of special preciousness and beauty, but linking it to a modernity which is necessarily that of the style you're seeking, thinking about and creating.

The embroidery of the Eighties was decidedly connected with show and spectacularity, an embroidery that tried, with its most typical and "evident" forms – from spangles to paillettes and jet – to satisfy a widespread desire to stand out. It was also fun embroidery but very much an end in itself. The embroidery of today and of recent years, contrarily, is characterised by its deep link with the reconstruction and revamping of what it has already been. Embroidery today is substantially an aware and personal question of style.

Which, as far as I am concerned, goes back to the late 19th and early 20th centuries, a period I dearly love, a period imbued with elegance. The glitter of embroidery or the opacity of embroidery, relief and decoration, had always been interpreted as a phase of elegance and refinement. Embroidery in my view is a question of elegance, fundamentally of aesthetics, and this is why my fashion design and embroidery are diametrically opposed to 1980's fashion and embroidery. VINCENZO DE COTIIS for HAUTE

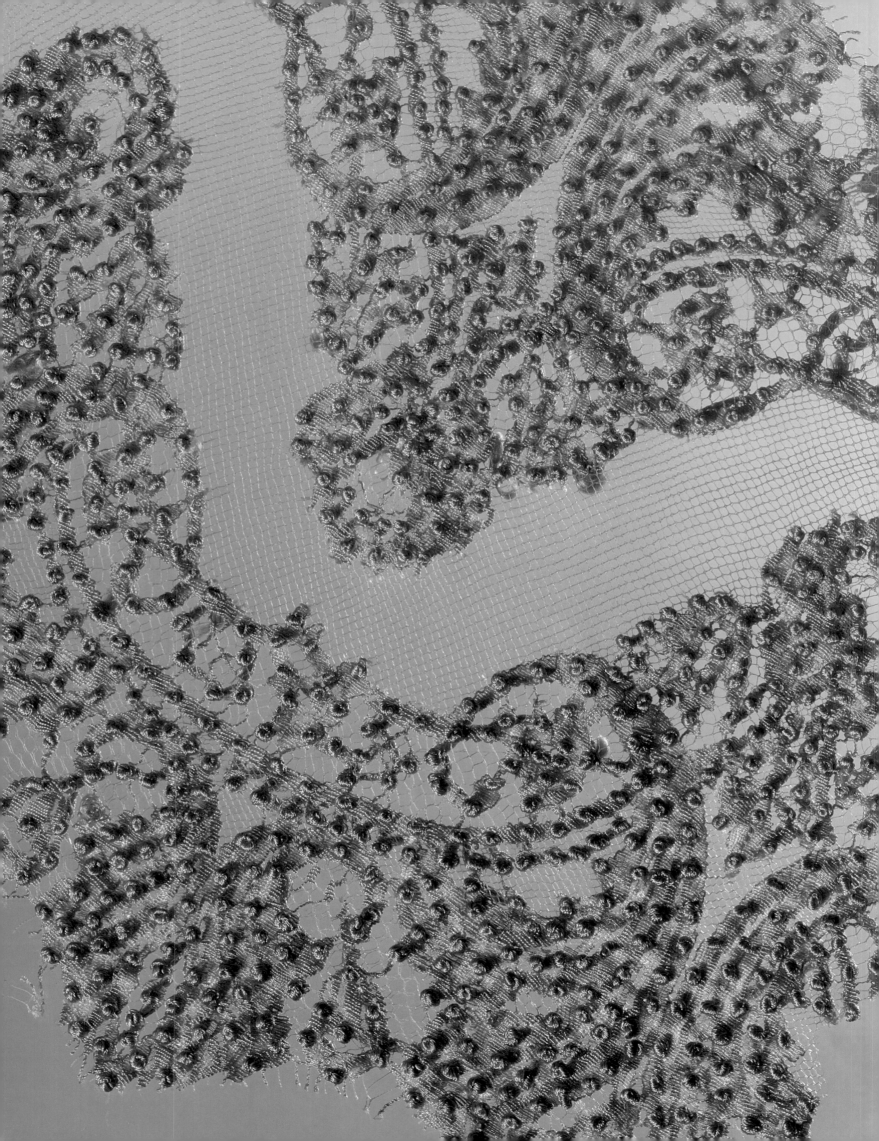

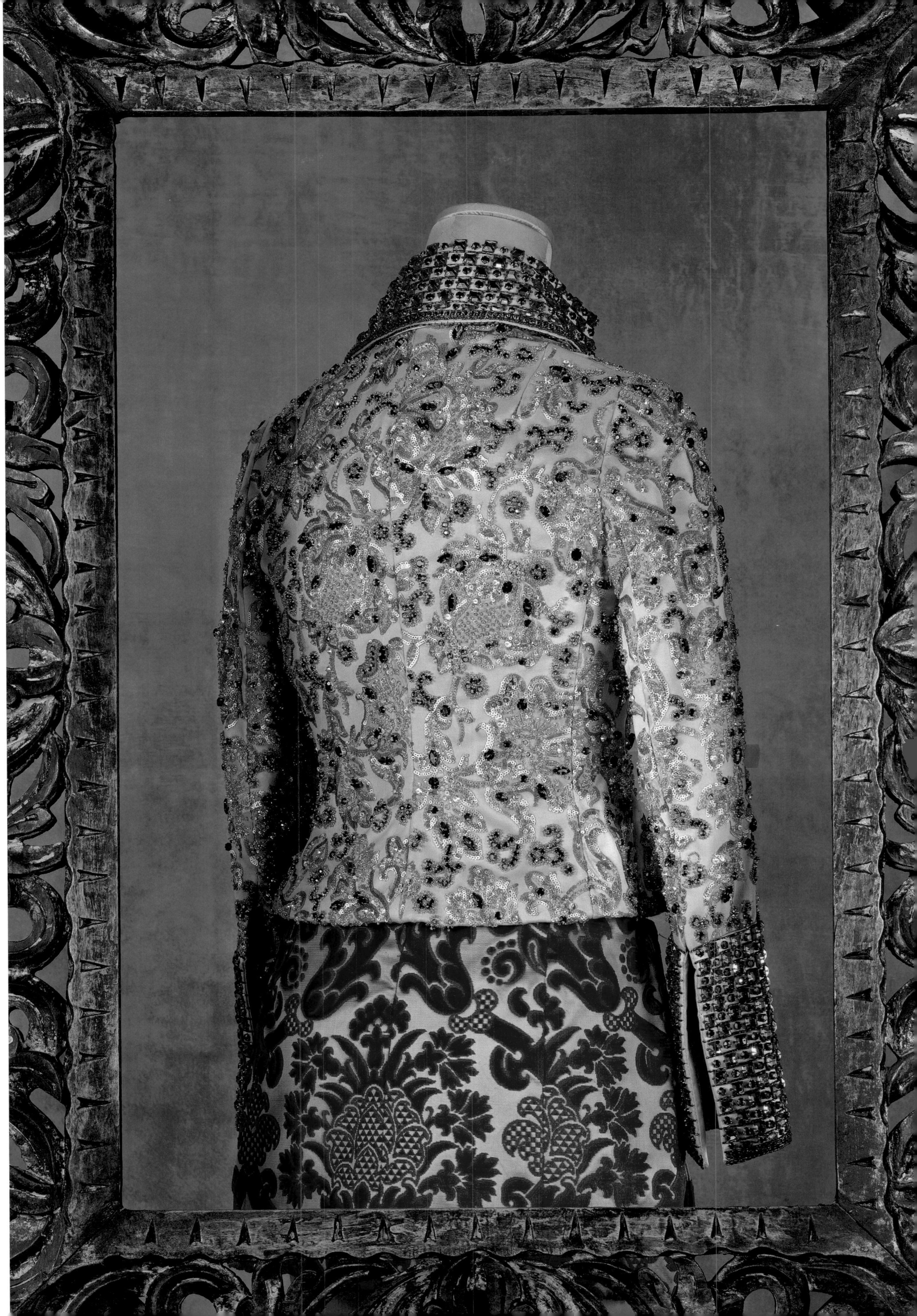

Dolce&Gabbana, s/s 2000

Craft technique, motifs and patterns, materials: I should say that the greatest attention must be paid to these three elements in order to achieve a unique result. Technique must be an expression of the finest expertise in order to fully ensure the desired performance; the designs must fascinate, attract and seduce; the materials must be of the highest quality.

Embroidery is virtuosity – meaning passion, skill, expertise – which generates emotion, enchantment, magic, dream… But embroidery is above all an art. And art calls for excellence.   GIANFRANCO FERRÈ

For embroidery, as for a dress or for a whole collection, inspiration may have different sources and courses: for example the figurative arts, the world of nature, cultures and ages distant from our own or a love of graphics… With this dress there's a direct reference to the kaleidoscopic principle of bajadere stripes, a theme dear to me which often recurs in my dresses, thanks to prints or the horizontal joining of different materials, which I also wanted to interpret with embroidery.

In some cases the search for an effect is the first element leading to the conception of a dress. In others the decoration is defined in a subsequent phase, as a response to the desire to complete the dress and make it special. This twofold perspective also goes for embroidery. With this dress, for example, embroidery is the essence of the dress itself. With many other models the embroidery maybe just discreetly marks a profile, veils a transparency, plays on cross references with a substantially sober and rigorous cloth, or adds a further touch of preciousness to materials already splendid in themselves, such as brocade… If I had to say it in a word I would say that in my collections embroidery plays a supporting-leading role. It's a versatile actor that can dominate the stage just as it can drop into supporting parts. An actor I'd never get rid of… In fashion as I practise it – which is not and will never be minimalist, or gratuitously ostentatious – embroidery will always play a determining role: as an expression of attention to detail and of a deep love for the most refined craftwork, which in my opinion are constituent elements of elegance and luxury. I believe that the aspiration to beauty is timeless and innate in the human DNA. And embroidery is a formidable instrument for creating, recounting and manifesting beauty…   GIANFRANCO FERRÈ

Embroidery is fundamental to me. I've always worked with it, right from my first collection. It's always been a point of reference. I've always thought of embroidery not as something only for glamorous evening gowns. I've never done great evening things with embroidery. I've always preferred to use it for garments that can be easily worn every day. I've always tried to use it with a more modern approach. I love embroidery because I love all craftwork, and in embroidery craft can be expressed at its highest level. I love using embroidery and application in contrasting contexts. For example, I often use antiqued Swarovski stuff that reminds me of very old things charged with atmosphere. But I like to use these things in apparently unusual, strange, incongruous contexts. My collections always include at least a dozen embroidered items: embroidery for me is always a point of departure and very often turns out to be one of the focal points of my collections.

My fashion design is always based on the idea of Femininity and Sensuality. The inspirational starting point is always more or less this, also with regard to embroidery. The cinema is one of my main references and inspirations, from neo-realism to the independent directors of today. I like the cinema. I like to draw inspiration from great women of the past, symbols of femininity and sensuality, but with the awareness that I'm observing them with the eye of the moment. I love Italian women above all and try to interpret their cinema prototypes in an international key: from the coolness of Silvana Mangano to the passionate Anna Magnani, my point of departure is in any case always an extremely strong type of woman.

With embroidery it's very important to me that the people I'm dealing with should be highly skilled, on top of the job. I need people who are extremely "ahead": Giorgia Rapezzi is such a person. I began using embroidery with her. And she has been a great help: she knew what I might like and she set me on the right road. She's the one who taught me to love embroidery.   ALESSANDRO DELL'ACQUA

Roberto Cavalli, s/s 2004

These two embroideries are highly representative of my work. They're called "hand burnt Swarovski explosion" and they embody something I'd wanted to do for a long time. I started out very young, at the age of twenty-four, as a consultant for various brands, and up to twenty-nine I had the good luck to always enjoy great independence and broad margins of experimental possibilities. Wherever I worked I was always given an 85%-90% margin of freedom to do what I liked. But I was never able to experiment 100%. Until the fateful day I made a trip to India where I discovered a wild world of embroidery. My first collection grew out of that trip which stimulated me to bring out all the research and experimentation I'd always sought in my career. My own boss, I experimented as much as I could. The Swarovski explosion was the result of my desire to see embroidery in a far more conceptual and newer way in comparison with the classic idea of embroidery and the Swarovski. I adore embroidery, I adore the history of embroidery, and I especially adore everything that sparkles. But I wanted to find a way to make something sparkle differently.

The "explosion" should be understood in the literal, scientific and technical meaning of the term. The Swarovski crystal emerges from beneath the leather; in some zones it forms small dunes while in others, gradually as the garment is worn, there's an actual metamorphosis of the garment itself: the leather is transformed, it opens up, it buds... the more you wear the jacket the more the Swarovski crystal emerges.

It's a type of embroidery I'm developing with Givenchy, and I believe it's an embroidery that will represent my style. Also with Givenchy I have the chance to explore and experiment with new embroideries, but my sign is the burnt Swarovski crystal and the explosion, especially from leather.   RICCARDO TISCI

I really like seeking and experimenting. Especially where emotions are concerned. Since boyhood, on every trip I've made, in every place I've been, I've always sought and always found objects, songs, photos, words… everything that aroused my emotions. And I kept these things in a sort of personal briefcase. I always told myself: one day, when I do my collection, I'd like to be able to draw from the briefcase everything that truly represents me. The bee, an insect I really like, is very closely linked to my style. I dearly love everything gothic and Victorian, and the bee was an auspicious symbol in Victorian England. I love bees for their colours and shape, and for the fact that the queen rules over her whole entourage of worker bees, if I may put it this way. I love that very elegant form of power. For my first collection I opened my briefcase and out came the following stimuli: the Victorian, the gothic and bees… to which were added Botticelli and A Clockwork Orange… My first collection was a mixture of different things. Some garments in that collection had bees which actually moved: the body and the head were made with Swarovski crystals sewn onto the fabric while two mobile crystal drops formed the wings. So when the garment was worn and in movement it was as if the bees were moving. Those bees gave me the chance to create something I'd long dreamt of. RICCARDO TISCI

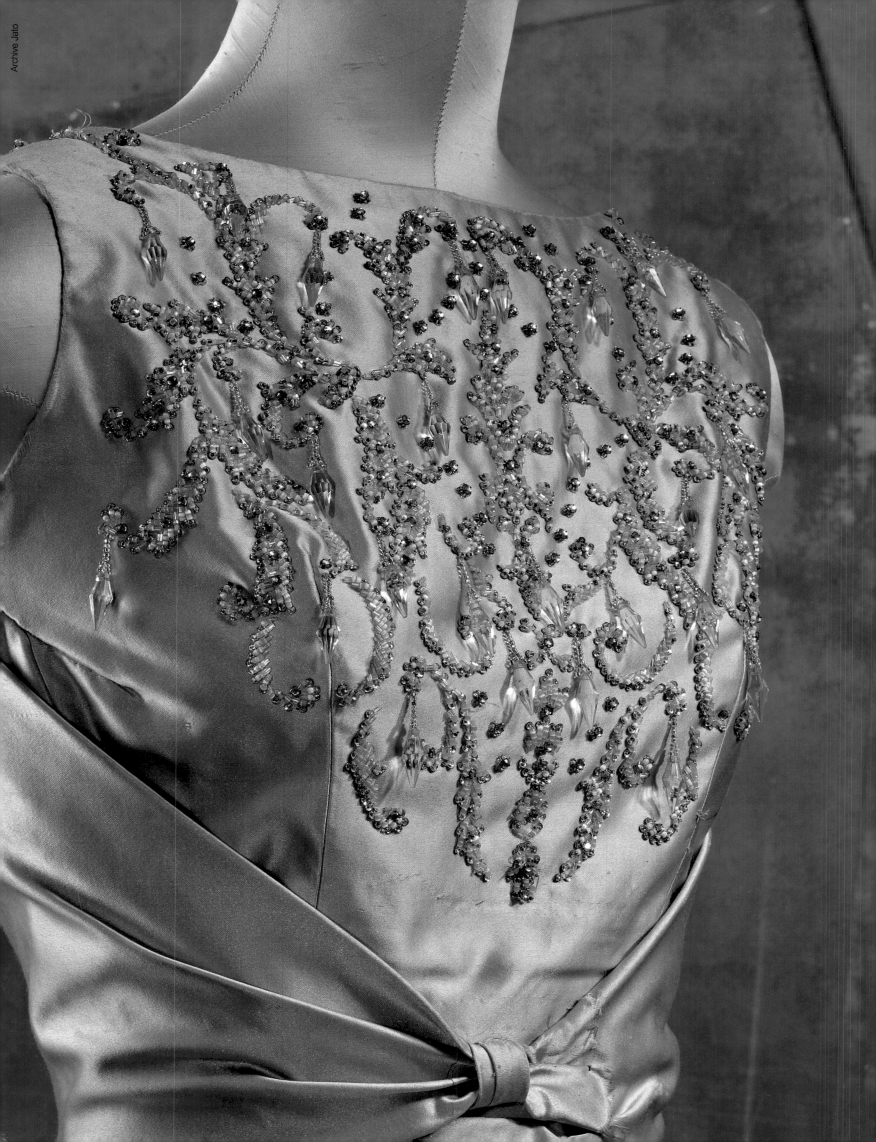

The basic idea, the concept and image we wanted to develop and go deeper into, was the rough diamond. I had a diamond shape specially made in Plexiglas and had it faceted by hand, irregularly. The aim was to create an interesting contrast between matt and gloss, a contrast typical of rough diamonds. I had these diamonds applied by hand to the bustier, alternating them with real rock crystal and Swarovski crystals. I also really liked the concept of contrast that arises from matching this very rich embroidery with woven horse hair fabric, a typical material used for the inside of men's bespoke jackets. I find a very elegant and chic contrast between the sheen/opacity if the ice-coloured diamonds and the grey of the woven horse hair fabric.

The collection to which this item belongs represents something of a turning point in my journey as a designer with regard to the use of embroidery. I began my career with widespread use of printed fabric enriched by applications to the finished product. It's a technique I've been using and studying for a few years. The 2005 autumn-winter collection purposely took on a definitely more refined touch. The embroidery in my previous collections was decidedly strong and sometimes even deliberately kitsch, because I really enjoyed the contrast between a print with a strong, even violent subject and delicate embroidery, perhaps with flowers in strass and rubies, which went somewhat against a collective image of evil that the print represented. I loved the fundamental contrast between positive and negative. This season's embroidery and applications however have a far more refined and retro look. We were inspired particularly by the Forties, by Elsa Schiapparelli, by certain films of the day. We did a lot of archive research into the materials used in that period. I'm generally very attracted by sharp materials. I formed myself on Thierry Mugler who often used slivers, sharp pointed things. Also in embroidery the aspect that most interests me is definitely the material. Having almost always worked with prints, which I then embroidered, it was always important for me that the material used for the actual embroidery should be unusual and above all capable of giving three-dimensionality and power to the cloth. This is why I've always concentrated chiefly on materials and forms rather than on the actual design of the embroidery itself. Also with this bodice, though it's fairly classic, what really interested me technically was, I repeat, the unusual material pairing of diamond and woven horse hair fabric. I realise that I'm increasingly fascinated by the possibilities of giving a garment three-dimensionality through embroidery. I like embroidery that "steps out" of the garment. It wasn't at random that I embroidered spiders on my dresses. I even chose this insect as my logo. I've often applied spiders with wire-cored legs to my garments, making them almost walk over the fabric. I like the idea of embroidery as a living object more than as something taken and "stuck" on the cloth.

I need embroidery to emphasise an idea, to give more strength to the theme of the collection. This is my conception of embroidery. This is the way I use it. Embroidery can be synonymous with luxury, just as it can be with refinement or even aggressive force. For my part, embroidery is the story I use it for and match it with. The embroidery of this top was intended – precisely like the collection it's part of – to be enigmatic and surreal, based on a series of harmonious contrasts. With embroidery I'm really more concerned about giving power and consistency to the story I want to tell in a collection. I concentrate less on the fact that embroidery may give a garment the allure of luxury rather than elegance, rather than refinement, or anything else people usually tend to associate with the concept of embroidery.

I believe, in a word, that the whole of embroidery and application serves only to give emphasis to what someone is wearing. Especially in a period like this where the individual's primary need is certainly self-assertion at ego and personality level in the society we live in. The need to stand out, to declare "I'm here, I'm present", even with an image or the collective imagination you want to identify with, has made embroidery and prints – and also a certain type of garment construction – increasingly evident and dominant in fashion today. I think that this fact explains the success that embroidery has been enjoying for the last few seasons. Of course some believe that the need to sweep everything away and go back to simplicity is making itself felt. But what seems to me undeniable is that people are still showing greater appreciation of elaborately worked, special garments rather than the clean rigorous ones of which everybody now has wardrobes full. We live in a society where our clothing has to get us noticed. Everybody wants to wear clothes that have a very strong psychological and communicative story. Just like in the Eighties when there was a form of confusion in society similar to today's. With the difference, perhaps, that those were fun years, people really loved enjoyment, and there were suitable opportunities and possibilities every day and everywhere, so a certain type of clothing was in line with everyday life. Whereas today there are less possibilities for having fun, there's no longer the widespread, contagious euphoria of those years. So it's normal that embellishment and decoration of clothing should perhaps have the function of "reconstituents", so to speak. It's probable that a fine embroidered dress is a "tonic" today, also psychologically, for the woman who wears it. It may also give her a stage presence, in inverted commas, more important and comforting than any minimalist age garment could give.

Without forgetting that embroidery, since its origins, has been a fundamental decorative element in the history of costume. I believe that no trend of any kind can erase this fact. ALESSANDRO DE BENEDETTI

The richness of the embroidery here is evident and immediate even to the uninitiated. I rarely make items as rich and flamboyant as this. My pieces always tend to be less obvious on impact: there's generally such refinement that from a distance you don't realise that it's embroidery. Also in my most recent collections the embroidery is almost always fairly soft, delicate and discreet. This was intended as a highly powerful glamour piece. We wanted to go over the top, so we filled it with Swarovski crystals, beads, fringes… everything we could.   MAURIZIO PECORARO

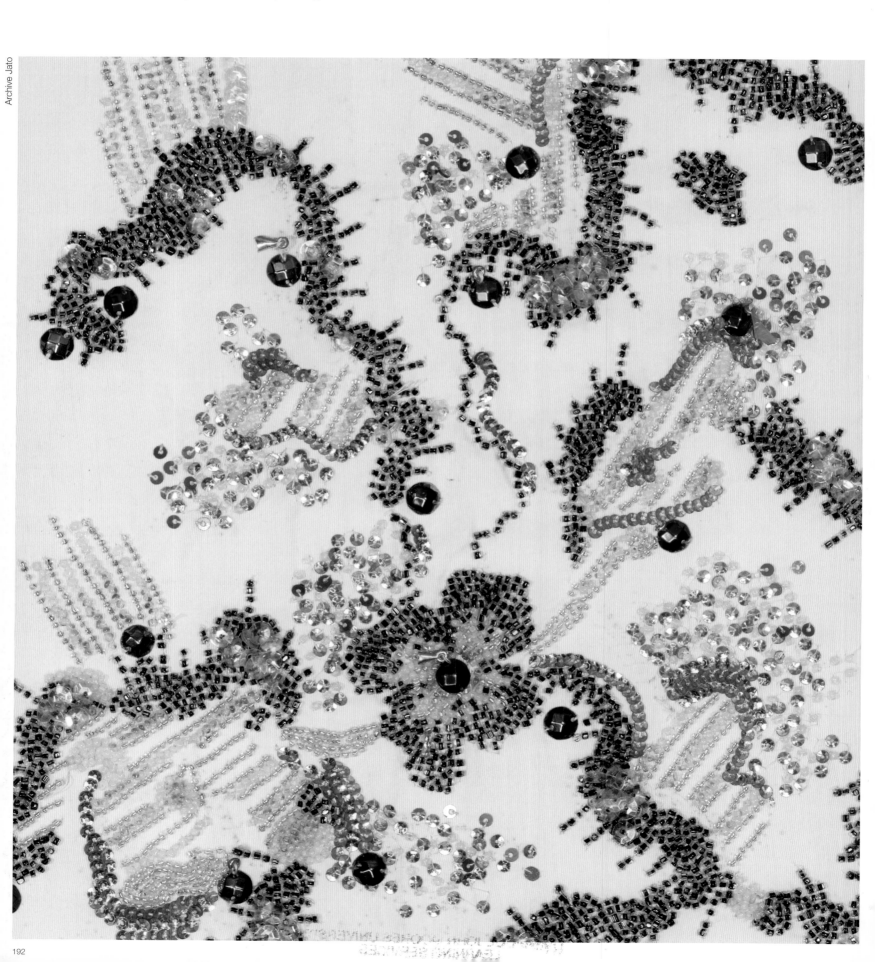

Roberto Cavalli dresses have always been characterised by research into colour and by special emphasis on sensuality and femininity. This is why the technique of embroidery is widely used, entrusted to top quality craftspeople who, by studying and researching materials and designs, create particularly precious and exclusive decorations. Embroidery gives life to a fabric through a play of light and shadow that enriches it with three-dimensionality and creates a powerful emotion which emphasises the dream of the person receiving a unique, refined garment. ROBERTO CAVALLI

I think that Etro embroidery could be defined as "cultural". The adjective "ethnic" is often used in connection with our brand and our way of interpreting embroidery, but I feel this to be a partial and superseded vision of our fashion design. The kind of embroidery I like is understood and interpreted in a modern way. And this doesn't exclude it from being inspired by ethnic groups and cultures other than our own. But there's no reason to speak of "ethnic" embroidery or style..

I like to draw on disparate cultures and cultural movements and then rework them into a vision that is as contemporary as possible. In this top there's the influence of Klimt just as there is the influence of the Russian tradition and of certain Venetian atmospheres... I tried to unite them in an embroidery that was also a jewel, that could enter into the garment and at the same time emerge from it three-dimensionally, and even surround it with the offshoot of the epaulettes in beadwork..

I really like the way Dries Van Noten uses embroidery. I don't think he's so far from our world. There's culture and research in his design and embroideries. He doesn't cover his garments with thrown handfuls of Swarovski crystals. That sort of thing maybe worked better in the Eighties when there were different needs, when women were different. In those days an ideal of strength, aggressiveness and power was upheld. It seems to me that other ideals are preferred now: good taste, balance, inquiry. Van Noten is exemplary here: in his embroideries you see a cultural journey, a high historical and artistic point of departure. But at the same time he always manages to make tasteful, wearable things.

In other ways I appreciate Jean Paul Gaultier's embroidery work, and I also like the way Prada uses embroidery though I find it extremely conceptual. It's often very "ahead", very modern and very contemporary. Prada uses and invents embroidery in such a way that it isn't obvious, and this is something I greatly appreciate. What I don't like are messy embroideries, the very "dirtied" or too "encrusted" ones, where an embroidery is superimposed on a painted part and maybe something else is added too... I like cleanness and balance. It's important that the law of order should remain in force even in apparent disorder. In this sense embroidery is certainly an art form, there's no doubt about it. And it's no accident that many have used embroidery to create works of art. I'm thinking of Boetti and Vezzoli, just to name two of the best known artists... But I feel there is still plenty to be done with embroidery in art. VERONICA ETRO

I really love embroidery, but the embroidery I like best is "recycled". This is the Haute philosophy. In my fashion design, embroidery must always be coherent with my way of thinking. I always like trying to revamp something that already exists. I like to recover and give new value to what's already there. I don't much like "reproduction", and that goes for embroidery too. Whatever type of research is carried out, and except in certain sporadic cases like this skirt, the piece is generally put forward precisely in the form of original embroidery. This embroidery was technically "feasible", reproducible. So also in consideration of market demand for this type of piece, we had it reproduced, in India to be precise.   VINCENZO DE COTIIS for HAUTE

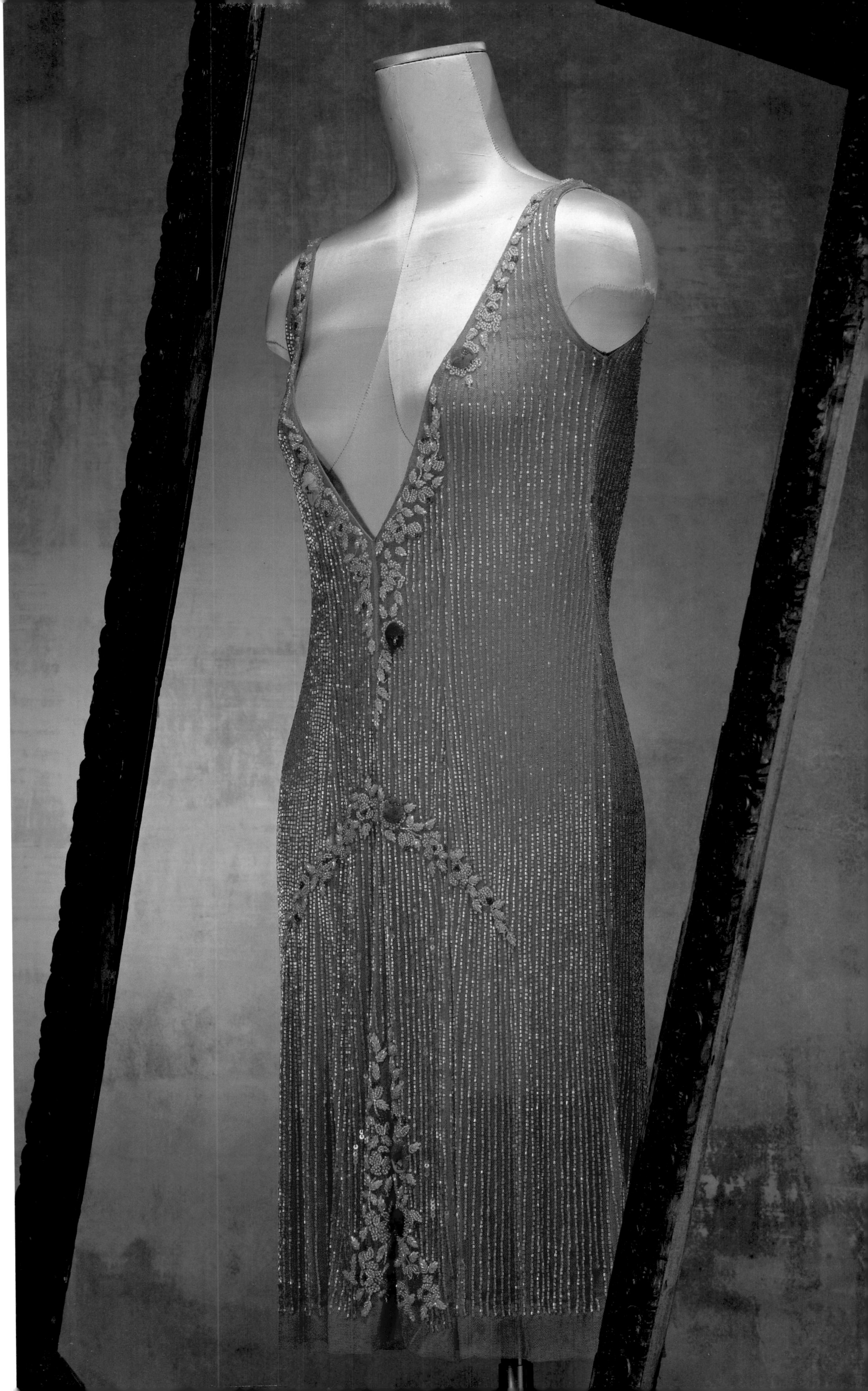

Blumarine, s/s 1999

The embroidery of this skirt is the evolution of a similar embroidery from the previous season. Little balls of chenille on tulle. This type of embroidery was much liked and I reinterpreted it the following summer season, putting touches of multicolour beads inside the balls of chenille. It was quite something to create. Technically really complicated. But it came out right in the end and I must admit that I seem to have done a good job which I like and which still gives me great satisfaction. MAURIZIO PECORARO

Maurizio Pecoraro, s/s 2003

Embroidery at the present moment loses reality if it lacks great genius. I feel we're going through a period in which embroidery is actually something superfluous, something added on. It's comparable to what was called "decoration" in the architecture of antiquity. Sometimes, if it is not more-than-designed and more-than-imagined, it may become almost banal, may become an "application". I don't like the reduction of embroidery to an application. I want it to be an integral part of the garment rather than something applied to it.

In my creations I set out from the idea of embroidery, building up a garment around it, just as often as I end up by adding the embroidery to the garment later. So it sometimes happens that an old piece of embroidery you've found somewhere gives you inspiration and leads you – through a process of personal revamping – to a result that may also be completely different from the point of departure. In these cases, when you find an object that especially fascinates you, it's down to your sensitivity as an artist to understand what stylistic elaboration should be applied to the thing you've found in order to make it modern and suited to the contemporary world in which you live.

Other times you may simply be taken by the desire to make a plain fabric more precious. So, fatally, you start looking for and wanting embroidery. In this second case the procedure is, for me, somewhat more difficult: I've more often been satisfied and fulfilled by work done on a find ("easier" and more "effective") rather than on the new.

I really prefer to do research into old embroidery, at the most perhaps also adding to it. I appreciate the values of fabric authenticity and handwork. I'm greatly fascinated by this aspect and my research is increasingly pressing in this direction, towards the vintage, the rediscovered, the old, while trying to avoid the redone and revamped.

What most fascinates me about old embroidery is certainly the technical aspect. Sometimes you find skills that have now disappeared and are hard to reproduce. But the very wear and tear of an old fabric also seduces me, far more even than the extreme preciousness of a new fabric: time, and the signs its passing leaves, have a great charm for me. I think it's actually the personal, intimate attraction which I feel towards a material that has experienced time and shows all the signs of it.   VINCENZO DE COTIIS for HAUTE

What I wanted to do here was develop an old English technique: the clothes of the "Pearly Kings and Queens". I'm fascinated by buttons. In embroidery you can use anything… even beer bottle tops if you like. Buttons attract me for many reasons. Once upon a time they could even be used almost as coins. Then there are mother of pearl buttons, hand worked in a complex and absolutely fascinating process. I don't know for what strange reason but I especially adore broken buttons… Using buttons for embroidery particularly stimulated me. Especially because I had the chance to somehow give nobility and value to an object in itself banal and everyday. I find that this process lies at the heart of irony, and as far as I'm concerned the ironic component must be absolutely present in my creations. This does not alter the fact that in the end, behind an amusing embroidery like this, there lies extensive research and study on the size and composition of the buttons, not to mention the considerable expense of the materials and their application. To all effects this is a very costly embroidery. But with two plusses: one the one hand irony and on the other the blending of banality and reverie. Anomalous use of the button elicits surprise. And surprise is another concept that greatly interests me. I like using materials in an anomalous and unexpected way: so in this collection I covered a jacket with buttons and overloaded a pair of knee-length boots, made of very thin threads of leather, with Swarovski crystals. I like to embellish, also with embroidery, unexpected areas of the body such as feet and hands. ANTONIO BERARDI

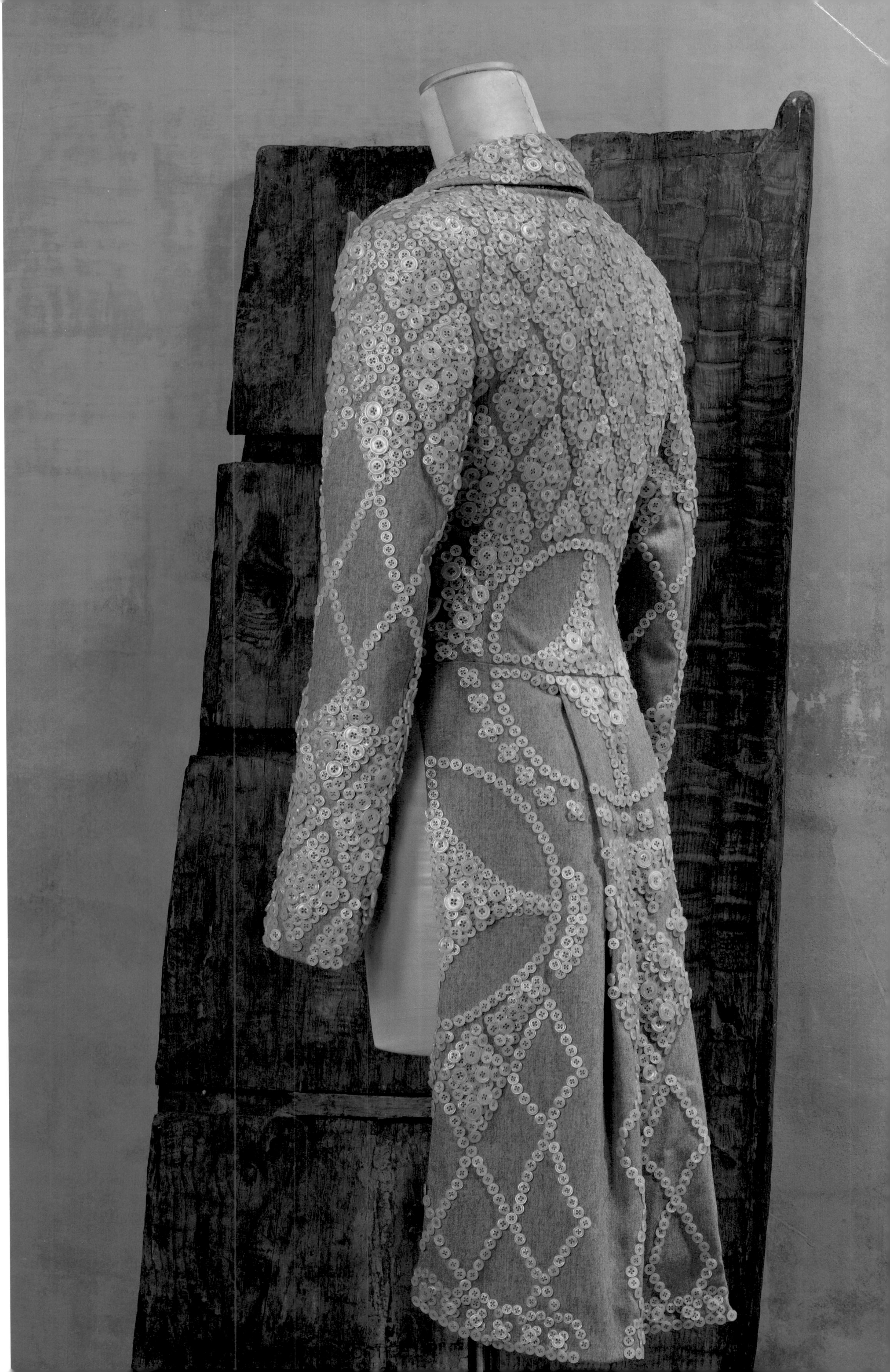

Antonio Berardi, f/w 2001

We experimented with material in this embroidery too. Here we have paillettes in leather, handpunched and laminated to best render the typical shiny sequin effect. This collection had an ethnic influence, or at least our conception and vision of ethnic. These motifs were inspired by drawings of decorations made on human skin by Sudanese women, scars produced by small self-inflicted burns. We set these motifs on tulle. The effect of the dress, worn on naked skin, somehow reprised the Sudanese concept of body decoration.

The fashion conception behind this embroidery is not very different from our first embroidered garments: the support is still tulle, the transparencies are still the dominant trait, the way you can wear the garments is still very similar. The fundamental thing is to succeed in making different themes your own and personally interpreting them.

Always giving a highly recognisable hallmark to the things you do is perhaps the only possibility we have of exploring constantly different and new avenues.   ALESSANDRO DELL'ACQUA

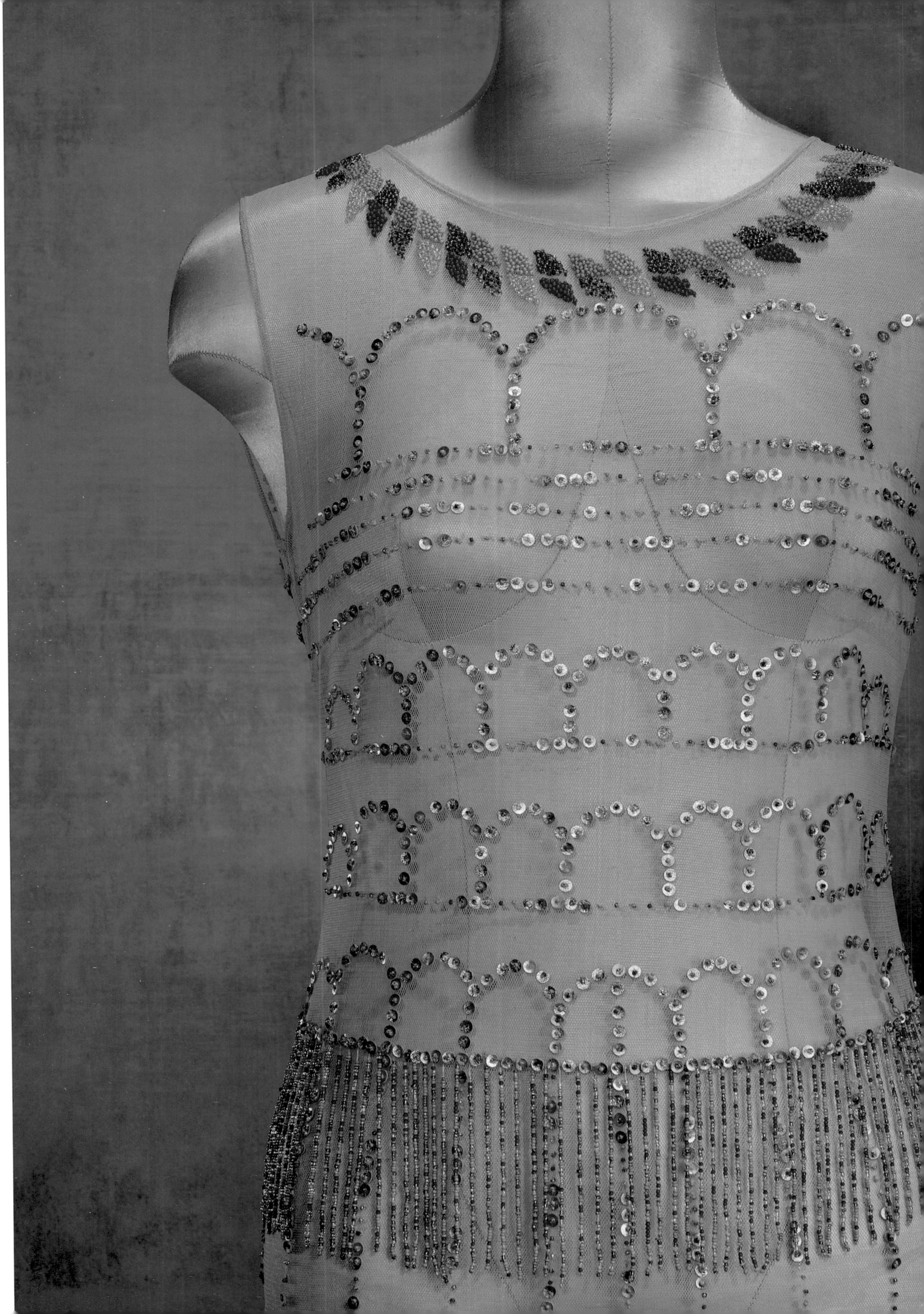

Alessandro Dell'Acqua, s/s 2000

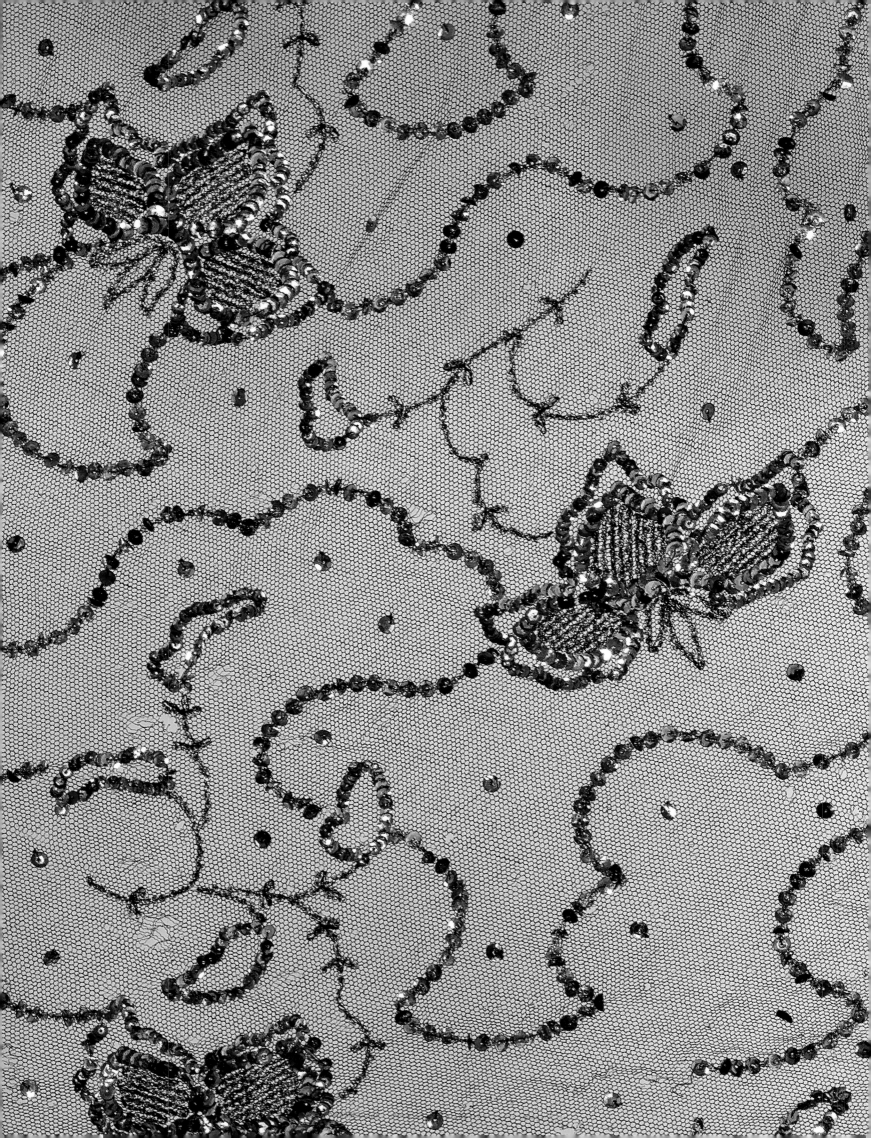

Minimalism struck the fashion world decisively, and for a certain period completely revolutionised the fashion system. But it had the defect of not being Dream. At a certain point people refused to go on with that type of fashion. Unfortunately, however, we slipped into the opposite excess, ending up with the most total baroque. Today it seems to me that fashion is going through a period in which there is the right compromise and balance between these two contrary trends. We're returning to a certain kind of cleanness, though not to the most intransigent and extreme minimalism. I believe that in this situation we can pursue very stimulating and interesting research on embroidery and its possible interpretations.   ALESSANDRO DELL'ACQUA

Alessandro Dell'Acqua, f/w 1997

Riccardo Tisci, s/s 2005

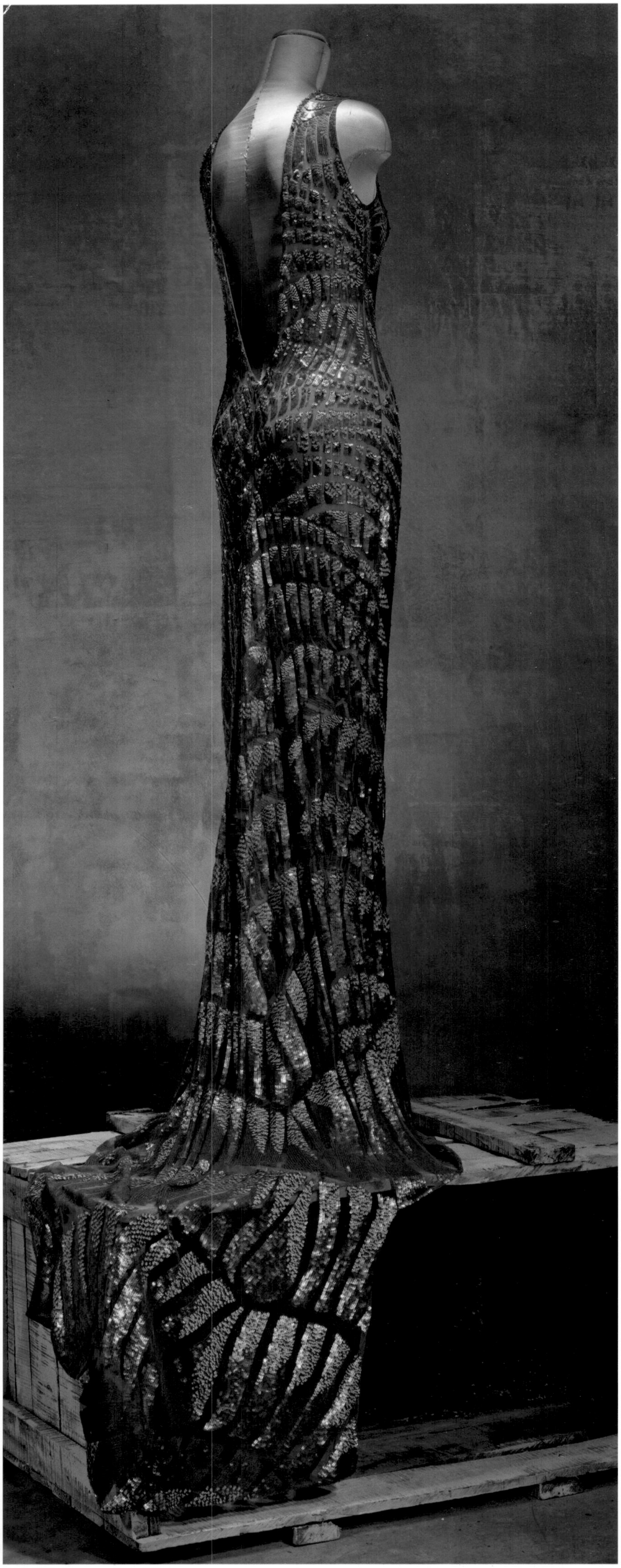

I like the fact that both emotional and technical virtuosity aspects cohabit in my embroideries. I'm a great extremist, I love black or white. I like to age things or, contrarily, polish them up. So I love either highly classic British style embroidery, all thread, or the more experimental, newer and more extreme kind, without limits. I love to try out burning, dyeing, destroying, covering… I love embroidery but in my collections you'll always find only two or at the most three embroidery stories at a time, whereas a lot of designers present fifteen or twenty. I only offer two or three. Before getting to the kind of embroidery which excites me – and which I hope will do the same to the beholder – I'm highly selective. I experiment a lot and of course I discard a lot of trials. The ones that remain and are taken into the collection are really special, they're little gems. I adore embroidery that moves, that makes a sound, and the kind that undergoes metamorphoses, that ages and changes with time. Its world is so vast that embroidery can be synonymous with various things. Up to the Eighties the use of embroidery in fashion had almost the value of a social phenomenon: those who could afford embroidery wanted to display a sign of power. A woman wearing embroidered clothes was someone who could afford a certain lifestyle and frequent a certain kind of society. Whereas with things as they stand today a marvellous thing is happening to embroidery, from two different viewpoints. On the one hand there's the business aspect: today it isn't only women who want to be embellished, since men too have begun to wear embroidered garments, thus opening up many new possibilities for the market to exploit men's fashion as well. Because embroidery is a sign of youthfulness, happiness, fun and emotion, and men as much as women want to be young, happy and full of fun... On the other hand embroidery as it is interpreted by many young people today can really do everything. Embroidery now dares to do things that once seemed unthinkable. You can even sew up a jacket with embroidery, and this is wild. It's something Azzedine Alaia invented for knitwear in the eighties. In the second millennium there are designers, whom I greatly admire, who make garments finished with embroidery. It's no longer the stitch that closes the article but embroidery. I think this is great. I'm talking about Galliano, about Alaia also in his latest collections for example... I find it very interesting that embroidery, once a very social thing, has now become something which in various ways, with different prices high and low, from couture to the youngest lines, really cuts through fashion transversally, at all levels and in all its branches. Embroidery has become an actual fashion typology. In the past there was the macro-typology of fabric and the sub-families of leather and knitwear, and embroidery was one of the many sub-sub-families, whereas today it is increasingly gaining importance in collections. To ensure the success of a collection a great deal is put into embroidery. You keep embroidered garments, they remain, they often have an inestimable value.

Embroidery went very well in the Eighties, disappeared in the Nineties and came back in the year 2000, but in a very powerful, elegant and varied way.

People say a new wave of Minimalism is coming back?... could be. But let's keep in mind that embroidery may have more clout in Minimalism than in Maximalism where it is far more shock than chic. Minimalism stands wholly on detail, and therefore on chic. Some people interpret embroidery badly. Because embroidery is not only Swarovski crystals. Embroidery isn't something you have to be able to see 35 yards away. It may be many things: a thread, a finish, an embroidered smear, an application on the handmade... I feel there's a very interesting aspect of embroidery in the Minimalism that's coming back in today. The conceptual aspect so to speak. Personally I too believe that "glitter in your face" embroidery is losing importance somewhat... But another side of embroidery, much more delicate and sophisticated, is increasingly on the up and up. In my view embroidery will go through an exciting period with the new Minimalism.

Embroidery in Riccardo Tisci's fashion design may be defined with one adjective: conceptual. I've heard this said, and I identify with it. RICCARDO TISCI

In the architecture of the past the actual structure of a building was enriched by decoration, which is to say sculptures and paintings that were genuine art. This concept was gradually lost with time, and architecture had its own formation, independent and autonomous, as if sculpture and painting – meaning decoration in general – had in turn detached themselves from architecture. The same thing happened to embroidery which in recent years has lost its link with elegance and luxury. Embroidery has somehow freed itself. Today, at last, we can interpret embroidery as we like and as we feel: each according to his own style and taste, beyond over- specific references and constrictions.

Embroidery has freed itself but certainly hasn't "died out". It's impossible to suddenly abandon the past, the history of costume, tradition. This is why I believe that women today still love embroidery and rich, embroidered dresses. Just as decoration is still used in certain cultures, so our society is going towards a form of culture linked to the search for detail and therefore, in fashion, for embroidery. It's something that cannot be abandoned, perhaps also because at the moment there's no different decoration formula as an alternative. Embroidery is still very much a part of our culture and it is impossible to exclude it.

Though it's true that when there is an excess (as happened with embroidery in the past) there is then a reaction and a return to a kind of minimalism. This is what's happening today in the world of embroidery. But I also find that using a material in a proper, balanced way is the right road towards overcoming momentary trends and market demand. A fine, well-made article is timeless. Or better, it always has its own time and "justness". The same goes absolutely for embroidery, be it rich or "minimal". Evidently there may be, at the most, a fluctuation, a different curve of progression in the trends of the use of embroidery in fashion. But for people like me who are fascinated and won over by beautiful things, embroidery remains one of those things that have no fear of time.

I've got no precise idea of a hypothetical ideal embroidery. I'm fascinated by everything connected with the beautiful, with aesthetics. My garments individually and from time to time represent highly recognisable epochs. It may be the 60's just as it may be the 20's or any other period in the history of fashion. I don't like to overturn my points of departure. What I prefer is to revamp them in a vision that is as much as possible "a whole". I like a style that takes tradition into account and knows how to interpret it and make it new.

My embroideries already have a history of their own: everything lies in making it live again while respecting it. We may also, if we wish, use the word "recycling". It's a practice I like and one I also use when creating interior decoration. I try to retain what I find, without ever doing violence to it. This is why my embroidery succeeds in conquering more than surprising. VINCENZO DE COTIIS for HAUTE

I like to use my instinct in creation, also with embroidery. I never work on the basis of rationality. Embroidery inspires me, speaks to me, arouses my curiosity and seduces me only when it has a meaning. I may be struck by a special method of execution, or a strange positioning or a curious material... It's never the same aspect that intrigues me. But what strikes me always strikes my irrationality.

I'd like to think that a woman in choosing an embroidered garment follows her emotional impulses. I don't know if this is so, but with me it's the only way I can work. And it's also the only way I can choose the things that I wear, or better, that I buy. The same goes for everything that surrounds me, not only clothes. The things I choose must excite me in some way, and I hope that everybody else has this experience.

In the history of embroidery I think Yves Saint Laurent has done wonderful things, special and highly exciting; in particular, the things he did with Albert Lesage are extraordinary. Elsa Schiapparelli's embroidery is equally exciting and so are certain things by Chanel. From another angle I think it's also extraordinary how Comme des Garçonnes has succeeded in modernising application.

Embroidery isn't always an index and synonym of elegance. It may often be very gaudy too. I find embroidery gaudy when it has been done only to demonstrate how clever the embroiderer is. Doing something for such a reason is, to my mind, wholly mistaken and vulgar.

I feel that embroidery is rather a symbol of luxury, even when humble materials and methods of execution are chosen. When it is done by hand, when much time is spent devising, creating and executing it, embroidery is certainly luxurious. Even when the embroidery in itself is humble, it is often just pretend and the work is luxurious all the same. Because true luxury today lies in time, and any embroidery requires a great deal of it.

But to be really luxurious I feel that embroidery should not be treated as a luxury item by the wearer. On the contrary...

I've always used embroidery in an absolutely non-maximalist way, so I'm not worried about any return to the minimalist cleanness that people are starting to talk about. I've always used it as an accessory and as a way of highlighting a concept. So as far as I'm concerned I think I'll go on using it as I've done up to now. If I need to use it I will, without feeling out of fashion. Otherwise I might just as easily do without it.

Anyway I'm no great believer in this type of journalistic definition: Minimalism, Maximalism... I feel that certain styles always need embroidery in order to tell a story, while others manage to do the same thing even, or only, through leaving it out. Maybe what will change is the way of employing a means. Because embroidery is fundamentally a means. ROSSELLA TARABINI for ANNA MOLINARI

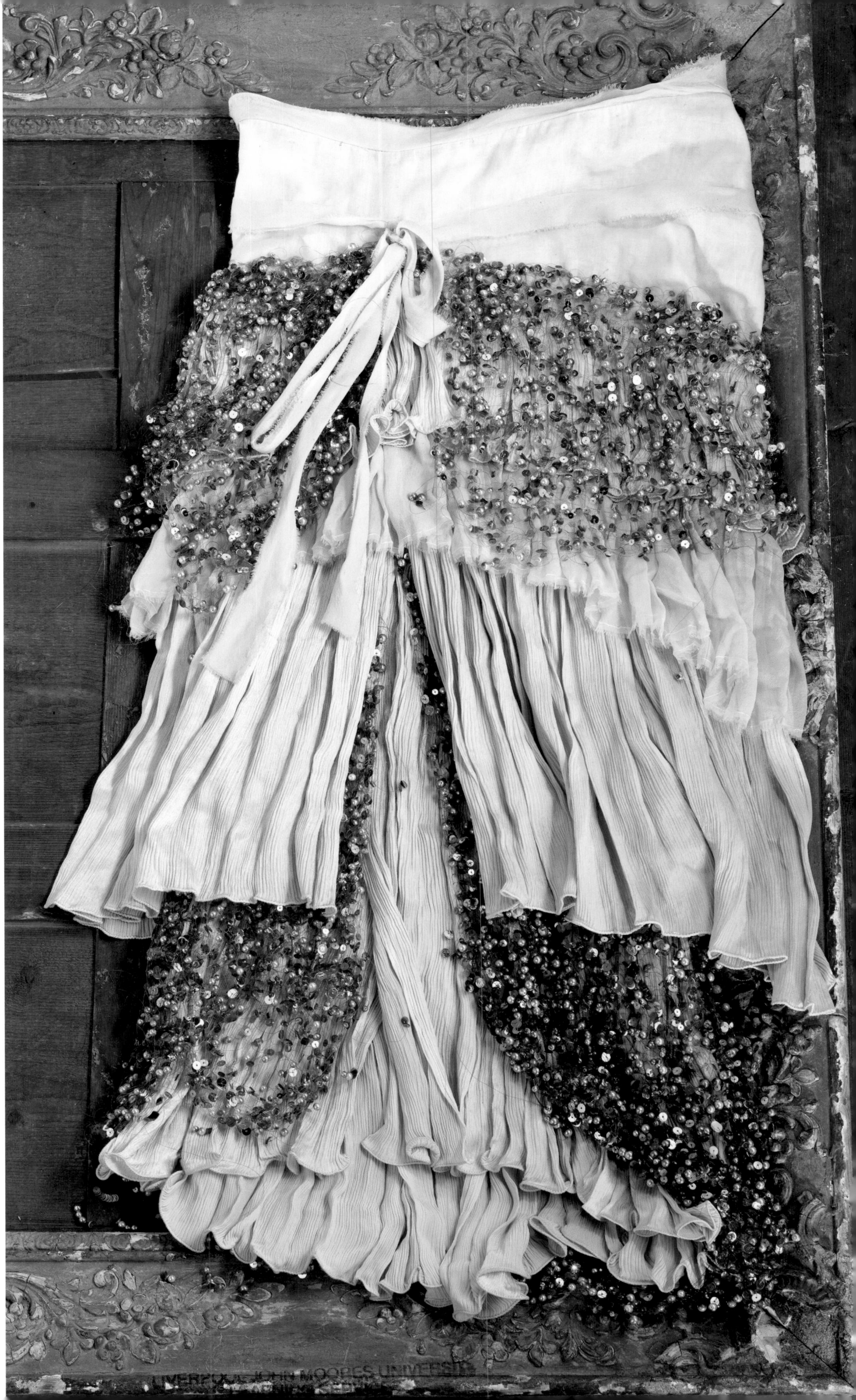

Anna Molinari, s/s 2005

My parents are Sicilian and I can't avoid loving the baroque. One of my mottoes could be: the more there is the more I like it. But for me embroidery is fundamentally a personal sign, a desire to say something. I use embroidery on a garment exactly as a kid might pin badges on a jerkin or a Tzigane stick feathers in his hat. Embroidery transmits a message, above all a message that expresses a

Antonio Berardi, s/s 2002

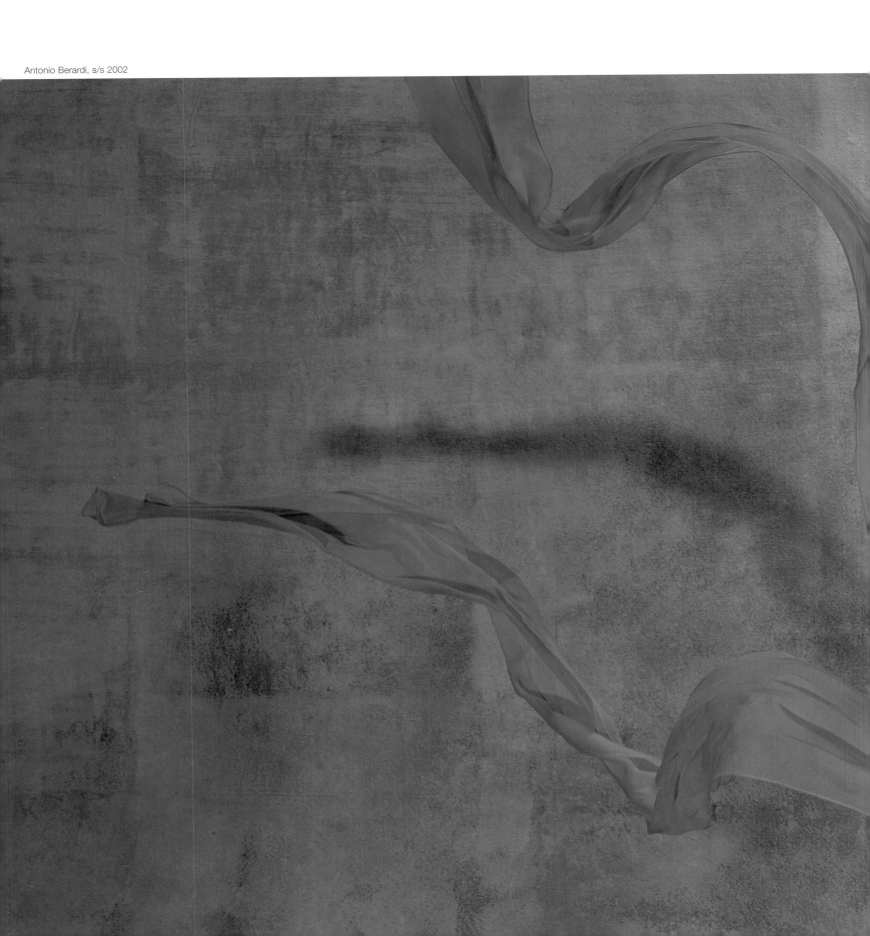

conception of fashion. But the great thing is that these messages can be infinite. I like the clearly and plainly decorative aspect of embroidery, but I also like the meaning, the sense that it may conceal. And if I'm asked, I love being able to reveal its secret, which is to say the message that embroidery aims to express. ANTONIO BERARDI

What most interested us here was to render the idea of paillettes thrown into acid, therefore completely corroded. We wanted the garment to seem like something taken (and immediately worn) from an old early century trunk discovered in an attic. Though apparently simple, the applied flowers involved considerable and difficult research.   MAURIZIO PECORARO

Maurizio Pecoraro, f/w 2001

In every garment I design – including modern or highly modern – I always try to put in all the elements of the history of embroidery that most fascinate or enchant me: little roses, macramé, the taste of the Twenties and Thirties (in my opinion the years of greatest richness, beauty and elegance) and the style of the 18th century…

A row of embroidered roses around a neckline, a macramé collar for a blouse, or a dress completely embroidered with vertical stripes in fairly strong colours, the whole softened and rendered elegant and romantic by little roses at the hem or the shoulders and the sleeves… all this clearly transmits my personal taste, which is to say my personality, decidedly romantic but with a touch of seduction. Because I think a woman should be feminine, seductive and romantic. These are three adjectives proper to the world of Woman, and I believe they can also be used to describe all my creations and my way of understanding and using embroidery. ANNA MOLINARI for BLUMARINE

Blumarine, s/s 2000

Working with embroidery means enjoying virtually absolute creative freedom. A freedom which printed cloth, for example, often does not permit, also due to costs. Using a colour placed print means very high implementation costs, whereas with embroidery – through skilful work of adjustment and composition – it is always possible to adapt a creation to a different garment or another model requiring a different placement.

This embroidery – clearly inspired by a Persian carpet – was of course done by hand. I feel that one of the most interesting things about it is the somewhat reckless positioning of the design, in the details of the revers of the neck and the scallop of the edge of the coat.

This coat dates to a period when we were using paillettes intensively, especially all over. I really liked and was very interested in the power and impact a garment like this could have. It was a phase of course, and like all phases it began to run out at a certain point. The great thing about embroidery is precisely this: you can use paillettes for a season and maybe use beads for the next, or you can go against the trend and use neither in the following season. With embroidery, understood in the general meaning of the term, you can always use and experiment with different work processes.

The paillette in itself is not a synonym of luxury; and vice versa luxury is not a synonym of paillette. The paillette is just one of the many decorative possibilities for a garment and as such its use is subject to the cycles of fashion. It depends a lot on the moment, the period. Right now I find there's less desire for paillettes, and I personally, in recent collections, have tended to use them less. Or at any rate more discreetly, with special positioning that gives touches of lighting effects in certain very specific parts of the garment. Nowadays I've got no desire for the all over, from head to foot. This doesn't mean that the desire couldn't come back after a couple of collections. As far as I'm concerned I like going through different phases in the use of various embroidery techniques. You can always experiment, manipulate, alter course. With embroidery it's like having a blank sheet where you can sketch out whatever you want. VERONICA ETRO

The inspiration was Leon Bakst's work. We took his prints, the spirit of the Twenties, the atmospheres of art nouveau, and translated them into paillettes in such a way that they would also be fun. The paillette lent irony to the sobriety, even the gloominess, of that period. VERONICA ETRO

Etro, f/w 2004

People today want to wear different clothes. A white shirt isn't satisfying. People want a white shirt with something else, be it embroidery, application or some other thing. Something that makes it different from the other white shirts in the wardrobe, the ones everybody else wears.

In this sense I like to think of embroidery in a very broad way. In a modern way. I feel embroidery should be understood as any work process that gives a garment added value, something that can also go well beyond stitched beads. "Embroidery" is any work process, designed ad hoc on a paper pattern, that enriches and completes the garment it is applied to. Even well-placed hand painting may be considered embroidery. An inlay may be considered embroidery. Lately I have much less desire to use embroidery as it is classically understood and executed. In my most recent collections I've used it more rarely, also trying to bring it up to date with inspiration from Matisse and contemporary art in general. Or I set the embroidery in anomalous and strategic parts of the garments. Or, putting my foot down on the extremism pedal, I replaced it with coloured Plexiglas spheres inserted in the dress, in belts or other details of the garment. Embroidery becomes application, detail, jewel. Hand painting is embroidery. Jacquard or devoree velvet can be embroidery. Even a colour placed print can give the illusion of embroidery (just as an embroidery may appear to be a print)… Laser cuts can be a form of embroidery… It's difficult if not impossible to give up embroidery altogether, because it's the only means at a designer's disposal to give a dress both three-dimensionality and lustre. But it can sometimes happen that "overdone" embroidery deprives the garment of lightness and breath; it may happen that the embroidery towers above it, "filling it up" excessively. I think I've managed to find compromise solutions that can broaden the concept of embroidery and make it topical. I think I've succeeded in upholding my desire for cleanness, for putting forward something unexpected and countertrend. Maybe I've disoriented people who expected something identifiable with what's considered the "Etro style". At that precise moment I was a bit fed up with the ethnic, with Africa, with India, with the triumph of rich, elaborate work. We've seen more than enough of this trend and stepped over it. I felt the need to wipe my slate clean, to put that vein on standby and try something else. I tried to do embroidery without embroidering. Fundamentally, embroidery is a concept. And a great number and variety of work processes may come under the heading of this concept.   VERONICA ETRO

Bad taste never dies. Like good taste, I hope. There were excesses in the eighties which made those without eyes to see believe that embroidery was vulgar. The vulgarity actually lay only in bad embroidery and in those who abused embroidery. I've always felt free to use it whenever I want to, and I shall continue to do so.   VALENTINO

Valentino, haute couture f/w 2003

A determining factor in this dress is the desire to depict, in a manner both romantic and speculative the firmament studded with stars, illuminated by the moon...

I think that what prevails today is a desire for uniqueness and originality that leads to an emotional approach to dressing. A dress is now experienced as an instrument for manifesting yourself, your own personality, way of being and aspirations. First and foremost the fact that you are an individual in a global and standardised dimension. So the "object of desire" dress must be distinctive, special, must have something that arouses sensations in the person who chooses and wears it, exactly as it must arouse them in someone who sees it worn by another. And in this scheme of things it is natural to distinguish the dress with decoration, ornament, important detail...

Embroidery is the expression of a luxury which I define "substantial" and which, in my creative perspective, represents an indispensable attribute of elegance today. It is luxury manifested in the intrinsic value of the materials employed, in unique craftwork and the processes which bring together ancient skills – one of the foremost being embroidery – and high technology, and in the singularity of details that give the dress its exclusive something else...   GIANFRANCO FERRÈ

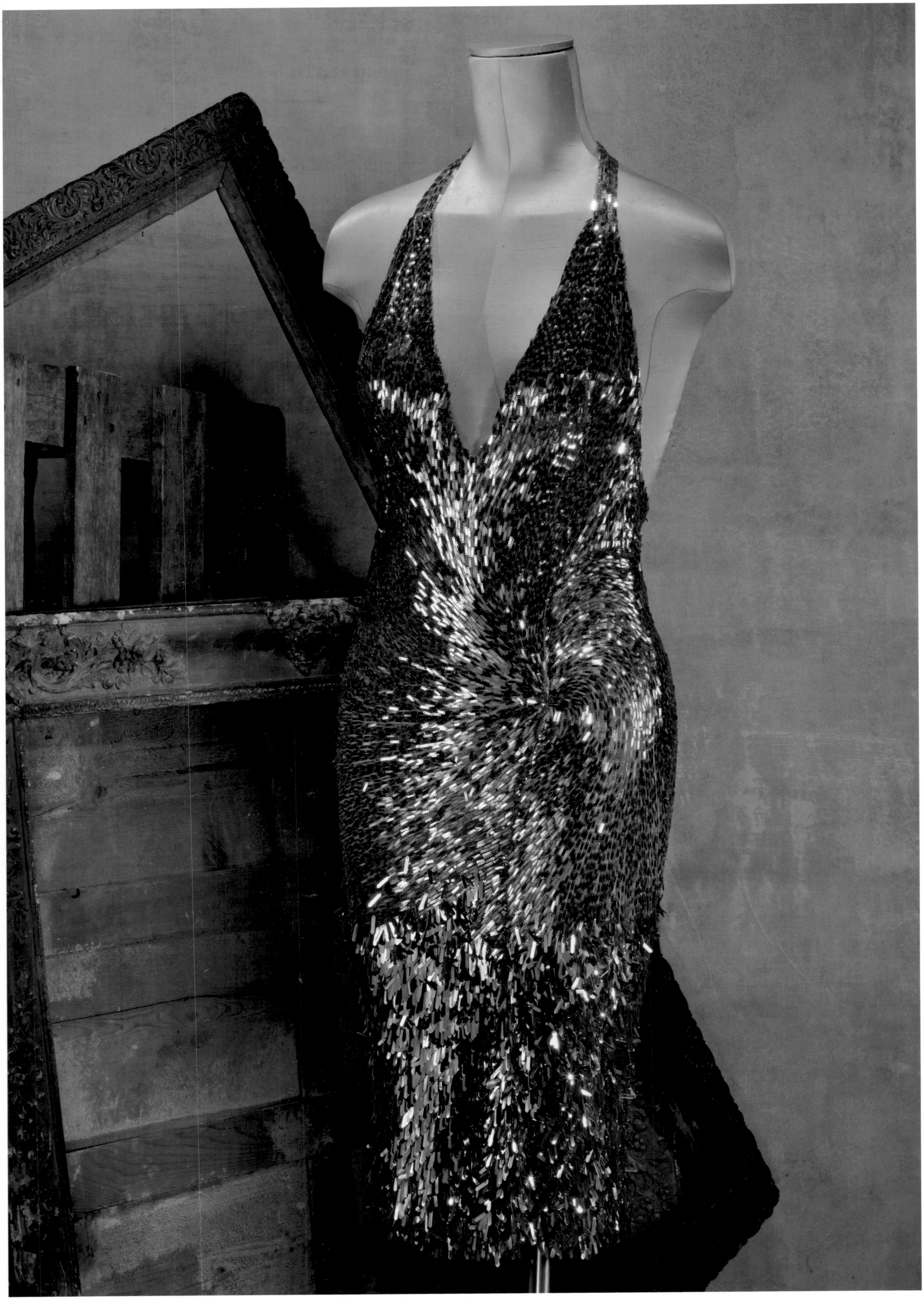

Versace, haute couture s/s 2000

Embroidery is not so much a question of fashion as of style. In my style, embroidery and decoration play a highly important and fundamental role: they are integral and indispensable.

Embroidery is a formidable instrument that you can use to dare, to please, enchant, seduce, give free rein to the most unrestrained imagination, even to exaggerated luxury. It's a battering ram for breaking into unheard of and unusual contexts of taste and elegance. It's a means of making the imagination concrete, of making a dress take on life, light, movement.

The decoration of a garment is often animated by the movements of the wearer's body. It thus acquires vitality, reflecting light in a thousand directions, capturing and fixing the observer's gaze at every step, every movement. It often aims at theatricality, at effect, the marvel of surprise. Often at extreme refinement of detail, at technical perfection, at impeccable execution.

Embroidery has no limits and imposes none. Embroidery is an instrument of freedom. I love using all kinds of material – the composure of geometrical designs as much as the anarchy of random disorder – and I love most of all to draw inspiration from any form of art or language that interests me. Music, painting, photography, dance, cinema. Yesterday as today. I love mixing stimuli and experiences from the most disparate contexts, fusing them into an amalgam that is always contemporary. Contemporary and enchanting.   DONATELLA VERSACE

A mistake is something I always like, also in embroidery: conscious and aware error and imperfection. I believe that all the embroideries on my garments are somehow imperfect. They are all errors. Errors may be something unfinished, something destroyed, something almost too vulgar or almost not vulgar enough: something that is almost dissonant, that doesn't correspond to the rule as commonly understood. I really go for this and am often misunderstood about it. In a thing that doesn't work, or works in an apparently wrong way, there is nonetheless and very often a thought behind it; it is never random. I detest harmony and seek only perfection in imperfection. I like the perturbing, the dissonant detail that disturbs and gives meaning to the whole. ROSSELLA TARABINI for ANNA MOLINARI

Anna Molinari, f/w 2001

I've never used the Swarovski crystal much. I may be going a bit against the trend but I believe that it's easy to fall into the trap of excess and vulgarity. Contrarily we were among the first and foremost users of the antiqued, the worn-out and the threadbare, also in embroidery. It has been a very important trend in the last ten years, but I think it's about to come to a close. Maybe there's less desire for the "second hand"; it rather seems to me that people want elegance, cleanness and "respectable" things. Maybe this tendency is a consequence of Italy being invaded by prontisti, black market criminals who copy the latest fashions. They offer well designed clothes, some highly embroidered or decorated, which are cheap but of medium-low quality. I believe that a certain slice of the market seeks quality, research and fine fabrics.   VERONICA ETRO

like to observe what's going on around me today, but I find equally that the past is an extraordinary source of inspiration. It cannot be forgotten or denied, and indeed the only way to keep going forward is to glance back at what has already happened. As regards the fashion world, there are certainly people who, in my opinion, have changed it and changed the way of dressing, not to mention my own vision of fashion. I like to think of Chanel who changed the history of fashion and costume. And there's another marvellous and extraordinary woman I infinitely admire: Miuccia Prada, who succeeded in making decoration an extraordinarily refined thing. This is what I like: to succeed in reinterpreting, re-elaborating and personalising decoration as Miuccia has done. Over recent decades the taste in and use of decoration have changed considerably. In the Eighties ornament was a motif of showiness, of belonging, of having arrived socially. It was the manifesto of a world. We are now living in another, different period, a phase in which decoration and the desire to wear jewellery again are something different in comparison with those days. I don't know why, after minimalism, men and women respectively discovered and rediscovered the desire to "decorate themselves"… I don't think it was a simple whim of fashion which must always follow each trend with a different one. At bottom, fashion is influenced by the reality surrounding it, somehow mirroring this reality and representing the times. Consciously or unconsciously designers are influenced by the world around them. Probably men just worked up the courage to wear things – coloured, embroidered, decorated – that were formerly unthinkable. At bottom I believe all this reflects the days we are living in. I believe, alas, that people feel the need to take refuge in things of a certain kind, including clothes, perhaps precisely to escape from an everyday life that they don't like. And the future? What I see increasingly is the need to create unique and unrepeatable things. We are experiencing a dangerous market situation with businesses being wiped out at production level. I feel it's important to create things which in themselves are unique, special, original and if possible irreproducible. People are attracted to unique things, and they buy them. People now have everything and more in their wardrobes. As far as I'm concerned I would like my clients to instinctively fall in love with the item they're looking at. I personally pause only in front of things that trigger my emotions, that draw me into trying, touching, looking at… and lastly possessing them. This is what I try to do, and I believe I succeed: to bring in irrationality. In appreciating an item one must see that it is the fruit of in-depth study and work, but at the same time it must touch off something instinctive that only manual skill – in which Italian fashion excels – can engage and arouse. Only the visibility of human intervention makes an article unique and therefore alluring. What I love is the evidence of the passage of people who, with their hands, have worked towards the creation of a dress. More than meeting a need, fashion must inflame a desire. At least the fashion that I like. ANTONIO MARRAS

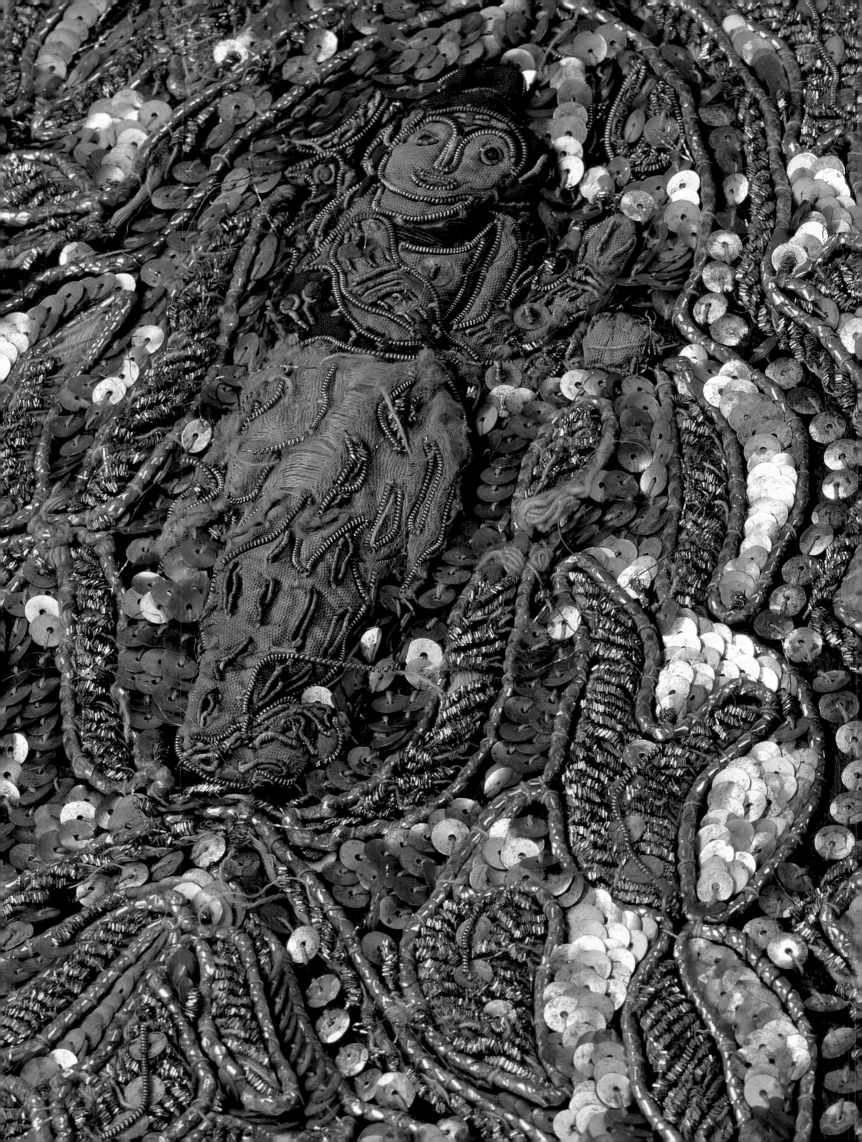

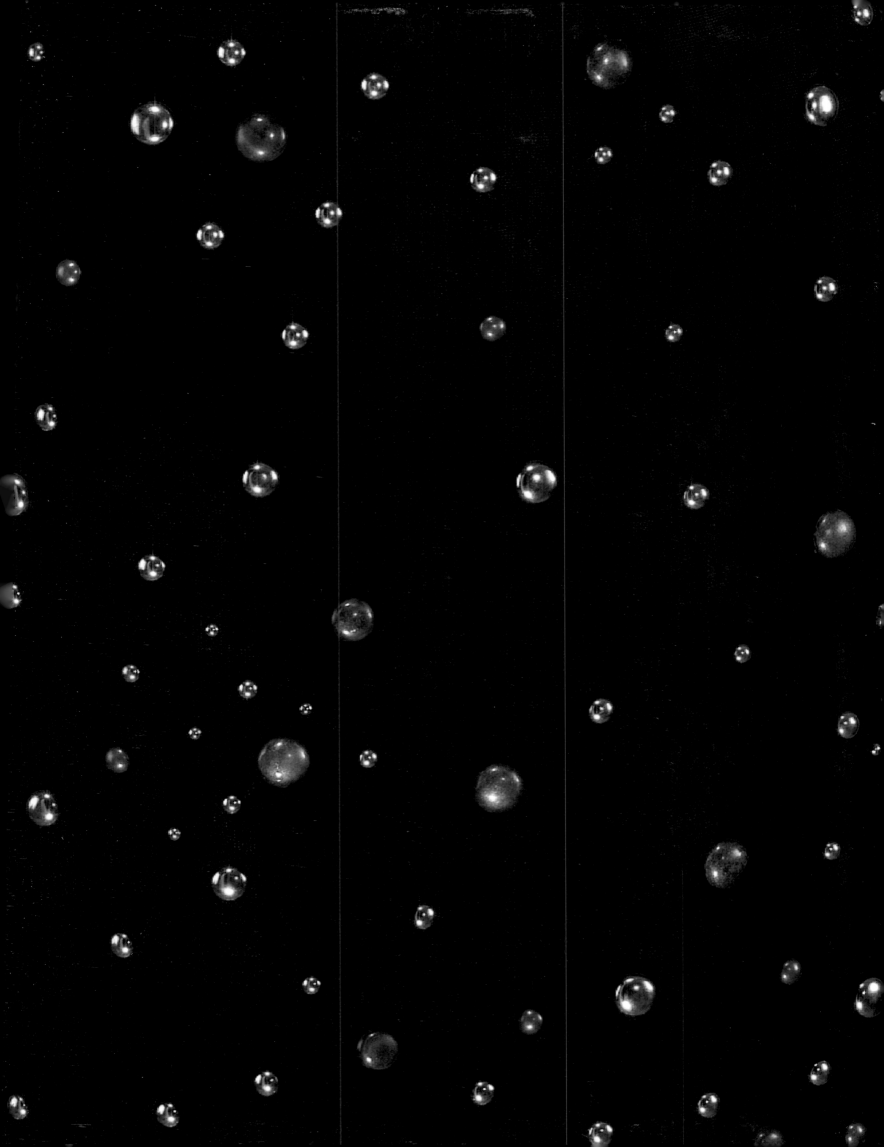

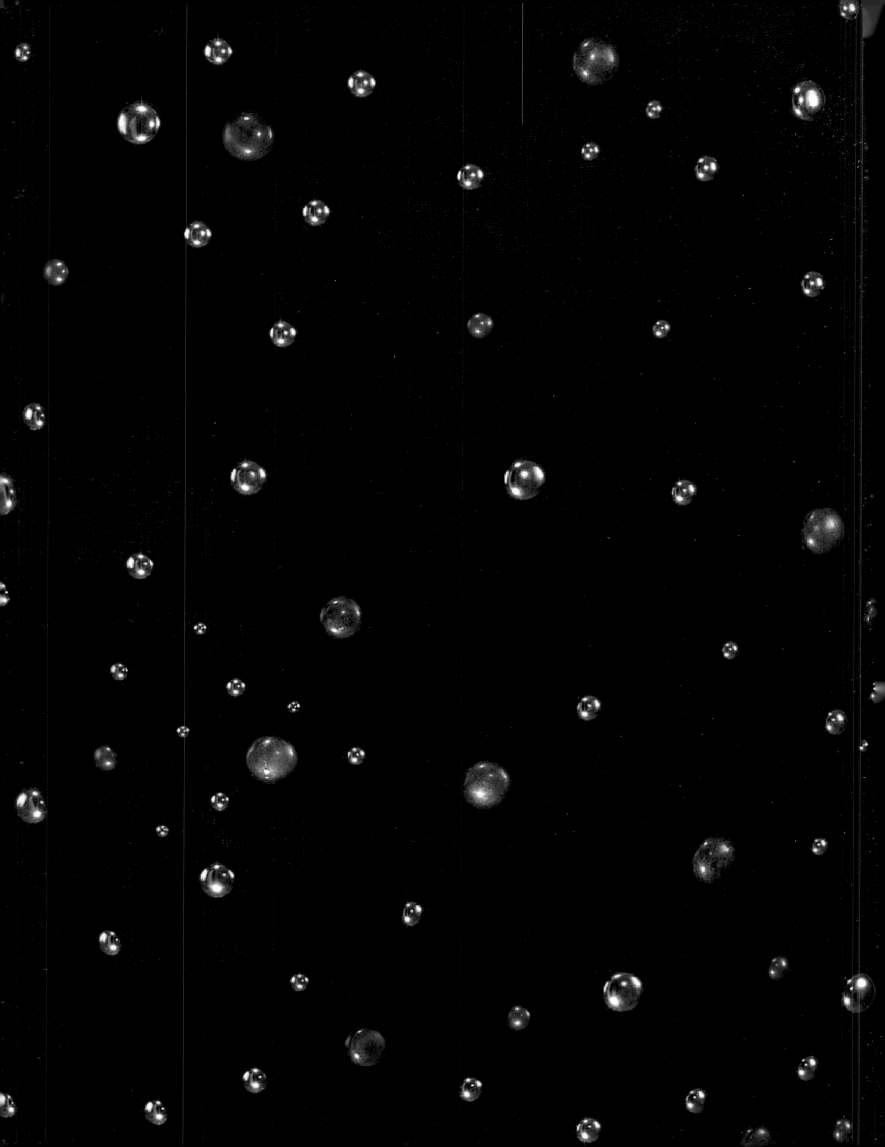

DOCUMENTATION

All the following pieces (except the garment on pag. 223 owned by the Blumarine archives) belong to the Jato archives. The autho[r] thanks Jato for kindly lending the garments and cloths photographed, and Jacopo Tonelli for the attributions and descriptions.

114	France, 18th century – Embroidery with silk ribbons and French knots in silk thread on a heavy tulle base
116	France, early 19th century – Embroidery with applied silk ribbons and silk thread
122	India, Early 20th century – Felt patchwork embroidery with stitching in silk thread
124	Eastern Europe, early 19th century – Woollen yarn and metal paillettes on boiled wool base
127	France, 19th century – Embroidery in silk thread on lace base
130	China, late 19th century – Embroidery in long stitch silk thread on silk damask
135	China, late 19th century – Embroidery in long stitch silk thread on silk base
136	China, early 20th century – Embroidery in long stitch silk thread on silk base
138	China, late 19th century – Embroidery in long stitch and French knot on silk base
145	China, late 19th century – Embroidery in silk thread and long stitch metal thread
146	France, 19th century – Embroidery with silk ribbon, applications in silk chiffon and silk thread
148	China, 19th century – Silk jacquard fabric
150	France, early 20th century – Embroidery in long stitch silk thread on patchwork elements applied to a raw linen base
155	United States, 1920's – Applications in painted leather, felt, metal paillettes and thread on a silk base
160	France, 18th century – Application of painted silk and silk thread on a moiré silk base
162	19th century – Beads, bugle beads, paillettes, silk thread, chenille, cotton and metal
169	Spain, 1950's – Embroidery with elements of lace and small disk, paillettes and half-sphere metal elements
172	Spain, 1950's – Metal borders and cords applied to a base of satin silk with paillettes and strass
188	Italy, 1950's – Embroidery in silk cut beads, paillettes, crystal and crystal droplets
192	Spain, 1950's – Paillettes, beads and metal applications
200	Italy, 1950's – Embroidery with strass, beads and fringes in Lurex yarn on a silk duchesse base
202	England, 19th century – Crochet
204	Italy, 1950's – Bugle beads and paillettes
207	France, 1930's – Embroidery of chenille balls applied to silk chiffon
211	Italy, 1950's – Flower shaped paillettes with paillettes, strass, beads and Lurex yarn on a silk base
215	Italy, 1960's – Paillettes and beads on silk shantung
218	France, 1920's – Paillettes and fringes of beads on tulle
223	1920's – Embroidery in paillettes and beads; kindly lent by Blumarine
226	France, 19th century – Metal thread, silk thread, painted silk and strass patchwork on satin silk
228	France, 1920's – Paillettes, beads, bugle beads and round-shaped jet of different sizes
239	France, 1920's – All over of paillettes with strass decoration
241	United States, 1930's – Floral motifs in beads and paillettes with striped paillette background
252	France, 1920's – Beads, bugle beads and strass
260	1920's – Leaf embroidery in paillettes and beads, with applications of the same leaves in paillettes and beads
263	France, 19th century - Metal thread embroidery and metal disk on damasked silk base, with application in silver, metal spiral material and various fabrics
268	Spain, 1950's – Metal disk, paillettes, strass
270	India, 19th century – Embroidery with disk and metal *spirale*, cord and paillettes, with patchwork application of upholstered fabrics
272	India, 19th century – Embroidery with disk and metal *spirale*, cord and paillettes, with patchwork application of upholstered fabrics

Printed in Italy, February 2006 by Grafiche Damiani, Bologna Italy